T0283644

Reflection and Reflective Spaces in the Early Years

Reflection and Reflective Spaces in the Early Years will support readers in developing their own reflective practice and creating reflective environments for the young children and families they work with. Combining case studies and reflective tasks to complement a range of theories, concepts and alternative approaches to reflection, this book shows how the reflective process can help practitioners adapt to rapid changes in the sector and improve professional practice.

Drawing on action research alongside the use of Japanese words and concepts (such as *Ikigai*, exploring your reason for being; *Hansei*, the art of honest self-reflection; and *Wabi-Sabi*, reflecting upon your perfectly imperfect self), chapters are full of practical guidance, activities and questions to prompt reflective thinking, covering such topics as:

- Reflection and Reflective Theory
- The Art of Self-Reflection
- The Reflective Underground
- Creating Reflective Spaces in the Early Years
- The Rainbow Researcher Framework
- How to Create Reflective Spaces in Early Years
- Exploring Creative Methods of Reflection

This book will be invaluable reading for Early Years practitioners, tutors and Early Years students on Level 3 courses and Foundation Degrees, but also for anyone interested in reflection or starting an academic or professional journey where you are required to reflect upon your practice.

Annie Pendrey is an educational consultant, lecturer and creative researcher in FE and Early Years and Education Studies. Annie is studying for her PhD and is the author of *The Little Book of Reflective Practice*.

Reflection and Reflective Spaces in the Early Years

A Guide for Students and Practitioners

Annie Pendrey

Routledge
Taylor & Francis Group

LONDON AND NEW YORK

Designed cover image: © oxygen / © Getty Images

First edition published 2023
by Routledge
4 Park Square, Milton Park, Abingdon, Oxon, OX14 4RN

and by Routledge
605 Third Avenue, New York, NY 10158

Routledge is an imprint of the Taylor & Francis Group, an informa business

© 2023 Annie Pendrey

The right of Annie Pendrey to be identified as author of this work has been asserted in accordance with sections 77 and 78 of the Copyright, Designs and Patents Act 1988.

British Library Cataloguing-in-Publication Data
A catalogue record for this book is available from the British Library

Library of Congress Cataloging-in-Publication Data
Names: Pendrey, Annie, author.
Title: Reflection and reflective spaces in the early years : a guide for students and practitioners / Annie Pendrey.
Description: Abingdon, Oxon ; New York, NY : Routledge, 2023. | Includes bibliographical references and index. |
Identifiers: LCCN 2022059057 (print) | LCCN 2022059058 (ebook) | ISBN 9781032311876 (paperback) | ISBN 9781032311906 (hardback) | ISBN 9781003308522 (ebook)
Subjects: LCSH: Early childhood education–Psychological aspects. | Reflective teaching.
Classification: LCC LB1139.23 .P46 2023 (print) | LCC LB1139.23 (ebook) | DDC 372.21--dc23/eng/20230221
LC record available at https://lccn.loc.gov/2022059057
LC ebook record available at https://lccn.loc.gov/2022059058

ISBN: 978-1-032-31190-6 (hbk)
ISBN: 978-1-032-31187-6 (pbk)
ISBN: 978-1-003-30852-2 (ebk)

DOI: 10.4324/b23021

Typeset in Celeste ST
by SPi Technologies India Pvt Ltd (Straive)

Contents

Contents

Acknowledgements

Book number two and another acknowledgements page!

At this point in my professional journey, I can usually be found writing chapters, blogs or working towards my thesis from the little corner of the house that is my creative haven. This is a space where my family supply me with coffee, my dogs snore peacefully and I type loudly (I do tap the keys very loudly). My circle of connections and animals are all integral to my thriving and happiness.

However, this book would not be complete without all the amazing contributions from the educators within this book who I have either previously taught or connected with through social media. All contributors have openly shared their experiences, and honest reflections, to support you in your reflective practice and professional journey.

Playdays Nursery were part of a 12-month research project for this book and, as well as the research, they keep my professional practice current and real, so a HUGE thank you to Lisa, Meesha, Sarah and all the practitioners, the parents, and the children too.

Then, there is my family who are there when I am talking to them about my ideas my reflections and my research. None of them are in education, so I know they nod and smile but are really thinking, 'What is she talking about?' Hopefully, this is not a phrase that you say as you begin to read my words, thoughts and reflections that always start with a fair few post-it notes but have now resulted in my second book.

Oubaitori – A Little Reflection to Start Your Journey

A little reflection as you start your journey. **Oubaitori**, a Japanese idiom that comes from the kanji, for the four trees that bloom in Springtime, these being plum, peach, apricot, and cherry blossom.

Cherry blossom and all kinds of Japanese wonders influence my work, as you will see throughout this book. But before you commence the many pages of this reflective book, I would like to invite you to consider **Oubaitori**.

To do this, take a moment to consider the world of social media, the environments in which you learn and/or work and how we might, at times, compare ourselves to others, or even wish we were more like other people in our world.

I would like you now to consider how every season you experience is different – from the chill of Winter to the extreme heat of the Summer – and how each season is unique, and each brings with it a different set of treasures and beauty.

Then focus more closely on Spring and the new life it brings. Spring also sees the explosion of cherry blossom, a riot of colour each year on every branch. It is only here for a short time, but every bloom on the tree is unique; each flower develops from bud to bloom at a different time.

It is here, I wish you to reflect upon the meaning of **Oubaitori**: this being that we all grow, develop, and bloom at different stages and so start this reflective journey with the mindset to not compare yourself to anyone else. This is your reflective journey, and this is YOU! So, as you begin this book, remember you are you, you will reflect, develop and flourish at your own space. Just be sure to enjoy the journey.

Travelling Through the Book

Chapter One – Reflection

In Chapter One, you will explore, what is reflection? What does reflection and reflective practice mean and how and why reflection is important in your everyday professional practice?

You will be invited to consider how reflection is a process not to be rushed as you begin to discover you are as an individual and as a professional. Moreover, you will begin to consider your professional curiosity, before reflecting upon how as individuals and professionals we are **perfectly imperfect 'wabi sabi'** and how this might impact upon your mind-set and professional practice.

In the final part of the chapter, you will be introduced to the Kawa River, a model you may wish to use to reflect upon your ongoing, reflective journey which may have obstacles and challenges along the way.

Chapter Two – The Art of Self Reflection

Chapter 2 will extend your reflective vocabulary with words such as **Hansei**, defined as the art of honest self-reflection or introspection as well as inviting you to explore how to use the pillars and rules of Ikigai (your reason for being) in both your professional or personal life.

Chapter Three – Reflective Theory and Reflective Practice

In this chapter, you will be introduced to several reflective theories and encouraged to link reflective theory to the reality of your everyday practice. The chapter begins with asking the reader to visualise their reflections and the use of reflective theory as a train journey where the train stops at different stations. You will be introduced to several reflective theorists such as Brookfield, Schon,

Gibbs and Kolb and encouraged to apply these to your professional practice through questions and reflections.

Chapter Four – Reflection and Research: Creating Reflective Spaces

Chapter 4 is an introduction to a 12-month research project with Playdays Nursery considering how to create a reflective environment. In this chapter, you will be able to explore how using the Rainbow Researcher Framework, practitioners reflected upon their professional capacity, used their professional curiosity and research skills to create a reflective space for the children in their care: The Blossom Room. The emerging results and the rhizomatic effect of the Blossom Room will hopefully encourage you to reflect and create your own bespoke reflective space within your setting.

Chapter Five – Creative Methods of Reflection and our Reflective Space

For those of you who have read my previous book 'The Little Book of Reflective Practice' you will appreciate my creative and reflective approach to teaching and learning. In Chapter Five, I expand upon this area of my work and introduce you to how creativity can support your reflective journaling and reflective practice. In this chapter, I will be sharing several creative methods of reflection and encouraging you to consider how you might use one or all of these at some point in your academic/professional journey.

The chapter ends with a return to *'wabi-sabi'* and how as educators our reflective spaces can also be perfectly imperfect, especiatlly in a world where we strive to be more sustainable. We can be sustainable and *perfectly imperfect*.

Introduction

Having started my career in Early Years many years ago, it was only when I began teaching that I discovered my fascination for reflection and reflective theory. It is fair to say it was whilst teaching that I began to appreciate how much pre-reflection is needed before any reflective theory is introduced. I often felt my learners struggled to reflect, embed reflective theory until I had spent time with my learners examining their personal and professional identities, their values and beliefs.

It has taken me years to discover who I am as an individual and, in turn, this has highlighted to me how every student, practitioner, assessor or teacher needs time and an environment of ease to discover, appreciate and reflect upon who they are as professionals.

Let's stop, pause and contemplate the following reflective questions before you begin the chapters of the book. Consider and try to answer the following:

- What is reflection?
- What is reflective practice?
- What is the importance of self-reflection?
- Do you have a reflective space where you can stop, contemplate and reflect upon your professional and personal identity?
- Do you take time to reflect upon who you are as an individual and/or professional?
- What are your values and your beliefs? How do these align to your professional practice and how do these impact upon your professional identity?
- How do you embrace your reflective activism?
- How do you create reflective communities for the children/students with whom you work, your parents and/or your colleagues?
- What challenges do you face and how do you overcome these?

Introduction

This book will invite you to reflect upon your reason for being, connect with who you are as an individual and reflect upon your professional practice. It will hopefully inspire you to be more creative in your reflections, support your reflective writing and urge you to examine and create reflective environments.

Reflection and Reflective Spaces in the Early Years is not only filled with reflective theory but also supported with research undertaken over a 12-month period with Playdays Nursery. Playdays Nursery is an inner-city private day Nursery in Wolverhampton and is open most days of the year to serve its local community. it was during the pandemic that I was fortunate to connect with the staff and embark upon the research that has informed my book, my writing and my philosophy.

How can this book help you?

If you are interested in reflection or starting an academic or professional journey where you are required to reflect upon your practice, then this book is for you. I don't ever claim to be an expert in any field, but I am passionate about reflection and research alongside all things Japanese, so I do hope that this book will inspire you to think and reflect differently and equip you with a range of ideas, theory and strategies for reflection.

So, if you are about to embark upon a reflective journey, have an interest in learning new words and approaches to reflection and wish to improve your reflective practice then this book is for you.

How to use this book

Within the book you will find two key icons, a blossom branch and a plant, both of which will encourage to stop and reflect upon a case study or a reflective task.

Reflective Task

The Blossom depicts growth and change. This is where you will have the opportunity to engage with some reflective questions. You can answer these yourself and journal your responses or it may be you work with others in a group, taking time to appreciate other's reflections, which may inform your own.

Case Study

The plant icon and its roots depict how, upon reading a case study within this book, it might lead you to new thoughts, new emerging ideas and support you in planting further seeds in your mind for you to reflect upon. Another word for this you might wish to use is rhizome thinking. Rhizome is best defined as a continuously growing horizontal underground stem which, at intervals, pushes out lateral shoots and roots: these shoots and roots being your reflective thoughts and thinking.

You can tailor this book to suit your needs and choose your own pace to work through the reflective content. In doing so you will hopefully become a more reflective educator who begins to consider how to create reflective environments.

Happy Reflecting.

1   Reflection and Reflective Practice

This may seem like a bizarre start to a chapter, but it begins with my own self-reflection and the start of my reflective journey into Early Years education. Let me ask you a question: do you have a drawer or file where you keep all your bills, either to pay or already paid, passports, paper documentation and generally paper-based things you may never ever use. Do you view some of those bits of paper as either personal treasures or memoirs? I do.

This drawer is where my NNEB qualification sits alongside my NNEB silver badge, which my parents brought me as part of my successful completion of the NNEB, awarded by the National Nursery Nursing Examination Board. This qualification meant I could work with children aged 0–8 years in a private or government-funded educational establishment. The title has since changed and they are more widely referred to as either a teaching assistant or an Early Years practitioner.

I will openly admit that I never chose to be a Nursery Nurse; it was most definitely a decision my career advisor pushed me into and eventually after an interesting conversation which included the following words I will never forget: 'You really do have limited career options with your parent's occupations.'

So, there it was. I was first advised to seek employment as both my parents at that time worked in a factory. According to the careers advisor they would not be able to support me financially. In part, this was true; we were most certainly not financially affluent. However, not a month went by without my mum taking me to the bookshop, having saved some money each week from her wages to buy me a book. She knew that reading was my passion.

I imagine that at this point you are wondering why this is important and relevant to the book. I believe these opening words and my careers advice experience to be my first educative reflection. So, upon sharing the words and my reflection on my careers interview, as a family, we agreed that I could go to college for two years, but that I would have to find a Saturday job to support myself and help my family and that's just what I did! Each Saturday and every

DOI: 10.4324/b23021-1

single day of my college holidays, I stacked sanitary towels, deodorants and nail varnishes in a small chemist, in addition to a job waitressing as and when I could until I qualified as an NNEB.

Back then in Early Years, we were called Nursery Nurses and our qualification meant we were qualified to work with Early Years children. I recall the course being academically intense and having placements in a wide variety of settings: hospitals, private nannying, nursery, day nursery, Special Educational Needs (SEN) provision and reception class. However, despite having to complete in-depth child development, observations, and essay after essay, I cannot recall a bespoke reflective practice module, or I may have just forgotten. What I do recall very vividly is listening to my tutors read my placement reports, my essay feedback and never really engaging in a reflective conversation. I recall once asking my tutor to place me in a setting nearer home, since I had to catch two buses and start my shift at the day nursery at 7:30 a.m. I was told to 'Get on with it'; not what I would call a two-way or indeed a reflective process. However, I loved my course and respected my tutors, and overall I enjoyed most of my placements. I even learned a lot from those experiences I didn't enjoy.

The world of education and Early Years qualifications have since transformed dramatically in terms of their approaches, their module content, the number of providers and the progression routes available. Moreover, our title of NNEB no longer exists. You may now hear the terms Teaching Assistant (TA), Early Years Practitioner (EYP) or Higher-Level Teaching Assistant (HLTA) to name just a few, all of which I am sure have studied reflection or been encouraged to become highly reflective practitioners.

I have taken an interesting and, at times, challenging academic journey during which I have become fascinated with reflection and reflective practice and its importance in the world of education to the point where I am today in my reading, research and writing. Teaching different age groups at many different levels has also given me the opportunity to consider what others, like yourself, might need to hear or read at the start of your reflective journey. So, let's start with the basics: What is reflection?

What is Reflection?

My initial response to this question is: reflection is honest, raw, and sometimes a little painful. What I mean by painful is that it can be challenging to suddenly openly share or become more self-aware of who you are as an individual or professional. Reflection is about being prepared to be open and transparent, with a willingness to share your reflections with others. All of these are skills are ones which you may need to develop; at this point, let me reassure you that you will develop all of these will in your own time. Try not to ever feel a sense of urgency to be reflective; by this I mean, if you are asked to give a reflective account but you find yourself unable to do this straight away then ask for time, pause, take stock, reflect, and return to the conversation. Reflection is a process and a journey.

To be reflective, I think you also need to be courageous, especially when sharing not only the small wins of your day, but particularly the challenges in your day or week. I also believe you reflect with your head and your heart, and that reflection is emotive; it can stir up many different emotions and feelings you may not have been aware of. Sharing your reflections openly and honestly within a safe environment can also be a healing process for some individuals.

For me, reflection is also a habit. It is something I now do daily without really thinking about it. I am sure there are many habits you perform each day of your life, from enjoying your morning coffee to perhaps walking the dogs or catching the same bus. A little like these habits, it is good practice to begin to consider how you can make reflection one of your habits, whether this be taking just five minutes out of your day to take stock and gather your thoughts and reflections or making regular entries in a reflective journal. (You can explore different ways to capture your reflections in Chapter 5.)

I also wish you to consider that reflection is not a 'bolt-on' to your course, training, or daily practice. Reflection and reflective practice should be an integral part of your daily professional and/or academic practice. It should be illuminating, like shining a light on your professional practice. It should be creative, supporting you to develop your confidence and be self-affirming. Reflection is a journey and so take time out, step back from the situation as and when you need to reflect. Most of all, I urge you to be curious about yourself as an individual and as a professional and also about the environments in which you work so that you can reflect in and on action (Schon 1983) and reflect forward, making improvements and becoming an agent of change.

The Reflective Process – Egg to Butterfly

As you begin your reflective journey you may wish to think about it like the stages of a butterfly, developing from an egg to a caterpillar to a chrysalis before finally emerging as a butterfly. As mentioned earlier, reflection should not feel like a rushed process; potentially, it is a process that may never be complete. Have you ever watched the stages of a butterfly? I have been fortunate to undertake this activity with my Early Years children and it was a truly magical experience. However, I was so impatient to see the butterflies and each day I would rush into Nursery hoping that this was the day that the butterflies would emerge; when they didn't, I was so disappointed. As discussed earlier, much like the stages of the butterfly, you cannot and should not rush your reflections; it takes time. You may feel just like the butterfly, but it takes time to find your wings.

Let me explain my thinking:

Stage 1 – Butterfly Eggs

For me, the butterfly eggs represent the very start of your reflective journey, perhaps the start of a new academic course or beginning a new job. At this stage, it is important to begin to consider when you will take time to reflect, either daily or weekly.

Having found a space and a time to reflect, begin to note down what your initial reflections are, any ideas you have, any concerns, any challenges and, of course, all the positives. The chances are you will need support during this stage: what support do you feel you need and how can you access this? It is so important at this stage to recall how reflection is a process and a journey and one which, much like the transformation from egg to butterfly, takes time and patience.

Stage 2 – Caterpillar

As you begin to become more reflective and/or more immersed in your course, there will be days you are very CATERPILLAR! By this, I mean you will have days where you feel you are just about crawling along and nothing you do seems to make a difference. The words you write may not appear to make sense; the activities you plan may not go according to plan and nothing is transforming. You really do feel like you are crawling along. It is at this point that I urge you to remember we all have these days, but in the reflective process this crawling is essential.

This slower pace is important; it is where you can become more curious about who you are as an individual, a professional and an academic. You should begin to reflect upon your values and beliefs in much more depth. Finally, as you know it is at this stage a caterpillar would be munching their way through lots of food ready for sleep and the transformation ahead. Just like the caterpillar, you too should be munching, but munching your way through literature, books and journals. You should be reading and engaging with reflective theory, beginning to consider how reflective theory supports your reflective practice and academic writing. (Reflective Theory is discussed in Chapter 3).

Stage 3 – Chrysalis

The chrysalis stage, the stage where you might think it's time to rest. I don't believe it's time to rest with regards to reflection, but it is potentially the stage where you can begin to slow down and take stock of your day, week or month. However, the chrysalis stage is where you should be engaging with wider reading; for example, wider reading around your subject choice and/or reflective theory, so that you are ready to begin the chrysalis stage of reflective writing.

As you begin to plot and plan your reflections, this stage is where you can begin to cement your professional practice to theory and log your reflective journey in essays, blogs, reflective accounts, or whatever type of assessment you are undertaking. This is the stage where if you have kept a reflective journal, your thoughts and reflections will start to emerge; you will be able to link your reflections to targets, actions or plans for your reflective writing.

Stage 4 – Butterfly

Finally, the process ends, or does it?

I would say reflection never ends, but for the purposes of explaining to you how reflection is a process, at this point you will be at the butterfly stage where you can begin to open and spread your wings. You will be transformed into a butterfly who is highly reflective and ready to start the next part of your professional or academic journey.

It is in this final stage of reflection that you will be armed with reflective theory and the ability to reflect forward as you continue your reflective journey. At this stage you should feel empowered to spread your wings, reflect and choose whichever direction your reflections have taken you.

Reflective Task

Take a moment to stop and consider:

- What do you now understand reflection to be?
- Why do you feel it is important?
- At what stage do you feel you are in the reflective process: egg, chrysalis, caterpillar or butterfly Why do you believe this to be the case?
- Are you aware of the support and/or access to literature and networks to support you as you start your reflective journey?

Keeping your notes from the reflective task, I invite to read the following case study from Nikita Phadnavis, an Early Years Specialist. I asked Nikita the same type of questions I have just asked you in your first reflective activity and this is her response after giving Nikita time to reflect. Her response is true, honest, and open: What is reflection and how do you reflect?

At first, when you begin to read it, you may think: what this has got to do with reflection? Read on and you will discover Nikita's new and emerging reflection.

Case Study

It's Thanksgiving Day in America. Amelia, a nine-year-old girl, goes to her mother in the kitchen to offer help. She sees her mother busy trying to cook a delicious turkey meal for the family. Amelia sees her mum chopping off the end of the turkey before carefully placing it on the baking dish, ready to go in the oven. She enquires, 'Mommy, why did you chop off the ends of the turkey?' Her mother replies, 'Because that's how your grandma taught me to do it. I learnt to cook from her.'

Since it's Thanksgiving, her whole family was luckily home. So, she goes over to her grandmother and asks, 'Grandma, why do we have to cut off the ends of the turkey?' Her grandmother replies, 'Because that's how my mother taught me to do it.' And she proudly continues, 'I learnt to cook from her, and I taught your mommy the same recipes.'

So, Amelia goes over to her great grandmother, resting on the sofa. She asks her, 'Granny, why do we have to chop off the ends of the turkey?' And her great grandmother replies, 'Well, you don't have to! The end bits are delicious, as they go all crispy.' Amelia is baffled, so she asks, 'But grandma and mommy said that you taught them to chop off the end bits of the turkey? So why did you do that if you think they are delicious?' So, her great grandmother replies, 'Well, you see, I had a very small wood-burning oven back in the days. It was too small to fit in the entire turkey. So. I had to chop off the end bits, as that was the only way to get the turkey in. Today, you have better and bigger electric ovens, so you don't have to chop off the ends.'

I had heard this story from my grandfather when I was eight. He taught me the importance of reflecting on what you do and thinking carefully about why you do what you do.

I learnt a lot from my grandfather, and reflecting, questioning, and analysing had almost become a habit. I would spend time over the weekends with my grandfather talking about my days at school, what went well, and why. I continued this habit even after moving away from my parents and grandparents.

But over the years, as I got older and busier, I started changing my habits in the hope of becoming more efficient. If something was working well already, I thought there was no need to reflect and analyse. So, I started using 'reflection time' only when things went wrong.

Analysing failure is a practice that is common for a lot of us. When things go wrong, we analyse what can be changed and what can be done differently. But when things are running smoothly, we don't usually see the need to reflect. Just like the mother and the grandmother in Amelia's story, they never questioned the process of cooking the turkey because the end result was good. They had a delicious turkey meal. But by being content with good and not questioning the process, they were not being efficient. They were wasting some turkey and missing out on the crispy bits. And this is how we may operate at a good level but not necessarily with optimum efficiency. My grandfather taught me this lesson: reflection takes you from good to great and great to outstanding. But unfortunately, I had forgotten this valuable lesson for the last few years.

Recently, I met Annie Pendrey on LinkedIn. Annie's posts on LinkedIn reminded me of my late grandfather. So, I decided to get in touch with her. We had an intriguing discussion regarding 'What is reflection?' I have worked as a Manager for an Early Years setting for almost a decade now, and I proudly told Annie how I support my practitioners to reflect upon their practice, not just when things went wrong but also when things went well.

> *Why did it go well, and what can you do next time to make it even better?*
> *What was the learning?*
> *Can you do it in any other way that can perhaps be more effective and efficient?*

I bragged about supporting my team to reflect upon the learning outcomes and individual children and their unique needs. I also talked about how I pay attention to the practitioners' needs, interests, and well-being. Annie asked me: how do I reflect? And again, my instinct was to reply by talking about what I do for my team as a manager. And that's when it occurred to me, I don't actively spend time on professional reflection, or at least not as much as I would like to, or I should be.

Managers, and especially senior managers in consortiums, don't always have supervision meetings or anyone to brainstorm with them. So as a manager, it is up to me to take the time to reflect upon my practice and my role as a leader. Just because things are not broken, it does not mean you don't need to replace them. I brought up this topic with a few friends who work across different industries, especially in senior roles. And although most of them agreed that the more responsibility you have, the more there is a need for reflection, most of them admitted to being guilty of using the 'busy excuse' – however, one or two who genuinely spend time reflecting, analysing and planning shared their experience. One of them worked as a senior scientist for a reputed pharma company. He had recently filed for a patent, and he gives credit to his habit of careful reflection. A process that had been followed over the years, he reflected upon his work and realised can be done differently.

That led to a new scientific discovery and the resulting patent. So, I asked these people what helps them take the time out for reflection when many of us have the busy excuse. A constructive tip that a dear friend shared was to make the reflection process exciting – something that you'd look forward to doing. So, he goes to a fancy cafe over the Rhine River for brunch every Saturday and sits with his laptop, reflecting upon his week. By associating a task with something pleasurable – the view over the river, the freshly baked croissants, and his favourite coffee – all make reflecting a pleasant experience. He does not do it as a tick-box exercise and hence benefits from it.

Another friend maintains a journal. He calls it is success journal. (It's not journaling, and he doesn't write everything. It's exclusively for success stories.) By default, we all focus on failure and things that went wrong to avoid further loss and embarrassment. We take pride in our achievement, but rarely do we reflect upon it or analyse what enabled us to achieve that success. So, he reflects upon his success and maintains a journal. He doesn't just document what he achieved and what he is proud of, but all the challenges he had to overcome, the strategies he used to overcome those challenges, the resources he used, the processes and the people who helped him. This allows him to reflect upon his strengths and analyse his performance and how he can improve.

Along with that, he creates a resource to visit when he is struggling. So, on days when he is not feeling the best or confident, he visits his journal, which gives him much-needed vigour and strength to persevere and reminds him of the strategies that have worked in the past. It also helps him feel better upon visiting his success stories.

Reflection enables us to stay on track. Because when we operate at high speed, it is easy to lose our way and go in the wrong direction. So along with speed, the direction matters, and it's the reflection and setting the intention that empowers us to do that. To begin with, it might seem like a waste of time, but sooner rather than later, you'll realise how much more efficient you've become just by reflecting on your work.

As a senior manager, now I get myself a box of cookies (actually, they are low-fat cookies) and lovely herbal tea, and that's my Friday afternoon ritual. And all of us senior managers in the consortium have agreed to meet over pizza (Dominos, not Weight Watchers) once a term to reflect upon our work and support each other. So, my first Friday session helped me recognise where I lacked skills and where training would help me.

I enjoy my reflection time. The half an hour, or sometimes an hour, that I spend with my cookies save me a lot of time over the week and month. It's not just experience that counts because there is no point being experienced at doing something wrong (or doing it ineffectively), just like Amelia's grandmother.

Reflective Activity

- What do you think Nikita has learnt about herself from both our conversation and by talking with others?
- How has she used others' lens to reflect upon her own professional practice?
- Why do you feel as individuals we may only reflect upon the things that go wrong in our day and life?
- How can we change this habit and begin to reflect upon our wins, successes and maybe even keep a success journal?

Nikita's case study reminded me that reflection is also about 'thinking outside the box'; to think divergently and invite others to be part of your reflective process. Asking questions of others, and asking others their thoughts, will support you in developing new ideas and approaches to your professional practice.

To summarise, reflection is a little like flicking through the pages of a magazine. Just like a magazine, each page tells a story, but you may pick one page to read and unknowingly review. This is much like your everyday life and/or your professional practice. You will choose a particular event to review or reflect upon. You will begin to question yourself more deeply, reflect upon your values and beliefs and, more importantly, consider wider social and political contexts and theories and how these fit into your reflection and reflective practice.

To summarise this section, I asked Rebecca Haynes, who started her career as an Early Years Practitioner and is now a Nursery Manager, the following two questions:

What is Reflection?

Why is Reflection important?

What is Reflection?

- *Reflection is looking at what you are doing and looking at how you are going to improve. Reflection takes place all the time, not only professionally but also personally.*
- *Reflection allows you to be able to highlight strengths and weaknesses to be able to then make strengths stronger and turn your weaknesses into strengths.*

Why is it Important?

- *Reflection is important because if something isn't working why are you going to keep doing the same things? You wouldn't surely? You want to change it, reflect why something isn't working and come up with a plan or a strategy that you can test to see if it will work differently or better.*
- *Reflection and reflective practice have been a big part of my career since completing my university degree. I encourage all my staff to 'get into the habit' of reflecting on a regular basis so that it then it becomes a natural occurrence.*

Rebecca's words highlight how as a leader she encourages her staff to be reflective. Reflective practice is whereby practitioners view themselves as researchers, thinkers, learners, and reflective activists. They go beyond merely reflecting upon their own values and beliefs; they consider wider societal and political perspectives, for example, and how these factors may impact upon their professional practice.

In the next section, let's examine what is meant by the terms reflective practice and professional curiosity.

Reflective Practice

Reflective practice first requires practitioners to look beyond self-reflection. Reflective practice requires practitioners to have an enquiring mind, to be curious and wish to seek answers to societal and political agendas. For example, a change in curriculum. Whilst it may be a document that encouarges us and guides us on how to deliver curriculum, a reflective practitioner will questions its content, and will be curious. They will not be resistant or fearful of change, but embrace it.

Reflective practice is about those 'head-scratching' moments, those 'Why are we still doing this in this way?' and not accepting the answer, 'Because we have always done it this way?' I have been in many meetings in my career where I have listened to people advise or tell me how to do something in my classroom. Often, I have sat quietly, as this is when I am in my reflective state of mind. I need time to digest words in a meeting and so often I am quiet and then I begin to process the words and wonder and question WHY? Why are you asking me to do something in this way? Then I begin to reflect more deeply, examine, and then verbalise my thoughts.

Let me give an example of reflective practice in action.

 ## Case Study

This case study is just one example of a piece of reflective practice from my career in education.

As a newly qualified teacher, I recall sitting in a staff training event about behaviour and listening to a set of rules that had been generated for all classes. The list of rules was not very long but they all started with the word 'NO'. I recall sitting thinking: Why do they all start with NO?

The list of rules continued and some I agreed with in principle but others I didn't. I began, for example, to think more reflectively about equality and choice.

Furthermore, I began to consider the wider context, which is part of reflective practice, my reflective practice and these were:

- *How will these rules support my relationship with my learners?*
- *Why do I need that rule in my classroom? How does that rule hinder learning?*
- *Will I be creating a power imbalance?*

I am not going to answer these questions for you as I feel there is more worth in you reflecting upon what you think or feel you would have done in this situation. Imagine, if you like, entering a classroom situation as a learner where the first session involves your tutor reading you a list of rules that begin with No, as opposed to an agreement or charter of behaviour the tutor and learner set as a collective.

As you take time to begin to reflect upon this scenario, I believe that reflective practice is very much about asking yourself these types of questions, expressing your feelings, values and beliefs. Reflective practice is about being open to change but equally challenging change too. Much like my case study, you too will be faced with professional or academic challenges so face them with curiosity, wonder and a reflective mind.

Professional Curiosity and Reflection

Professional curiosity is when you use your capacity as an educator and your communication skills to ponder, wonder, question and reflect upon your own professional practice.

Professional curiosity is a term I was introduced to as a degree student many years ago, and one which I recall, at first, made me a little uneasy in the lecture. I recall thinking about the term curiosity and honestly not sure what it meant to me in my capacity as a Nursery Nurse. I was often told what to do and how to do it in my working day when I worked in Early Years, and more often than not I was only ever allowed to have freedom with creative activities with the children. I honestly recall only ever being asked to design cards for every celebration in the academic year, so when asked how I was professionally curious and/or reflective, or how I created change, by my tutor, I must admit I had no answer.

Writing this book has stirred up many reflections about my role as a Nursery Nurse and how my professional status may not have been fully recognised, but I held dear to my professional responsibility working with Early Years children. I have since reflected upon and questioned how my professional curiosity may have been hindered by lack of recognition of my role, my status, and the hierarchal structures within education at the time. Furthermore, I have reflected upon how daily, without really thinking, I innately always strived for outstanding quality interactions with each child and introduced them to creative processes. I recognised then, as I do now, how often I reflected upon how I unknowingly, prior to my degree studies, I attempted to use my professional curiosity to challenge the constant 'product' creations, this being the card production line or every child having to do a painting to take home. However, despite my reflections, often my voice was unheard. It would have been easy to accept the daily creative planning and remain silent; instead I believe I strived to shine a light upon my professional practice and, in turn, create change.

I recall one specific event as a Nursery Nurse which became a turning point in my understanding of the term 'professional curiosity'. I was pregnant with my second child and about to start maternity leave just as we were about to break up for the Christmas break and the end of term. However, before I finished, the reception teacher I worked with at the time asked me to create 30 Easter cards. Yes, Easter cards! The cards were to be produced by each child and then popped away in storage until Easter arrived, when each child could take their card home. I began to think and reflect more in depth about how this activity would initially enhance a child's development in some ways possibly but, as the design was chosen by the adult, the materials cut out by the adult and then the child adult-directed, it really was a product rather than a process activity. I empowered myself to speak to the teacher and ask if we could rethink, change the activity, or indeed leave Easter until it was actually Easter, when the activity would mean more to the young children.

It was this event that witnessed the beginning of my empowerment, reflective and professional curious self. Sadly, despite a conversation with the reception teacher, I still sat and produced 30 Easter cards but there is a shining light. I believe that even when as educators we are in a situation where our voices may not be heard and our professional curiosity squashed, our reflections become more powerful. For me, I re-imagined how my class would be. I learnt the importance of reflective listening as an aspect of teamwork, and I took my shining light and took time to reflect over my maternity leave to carve out a new path and a new direction for myself.

Wabi-Sabi and Perfectly Imperfect

Having explored reflection, reflective practice, and professional curiosity, I now want to introduce you to the concept of *perfectly imperfect*.

- Stop for a moment and reflect upon how many times in your day or week you strive to be all things to all people.
- How much do you try to please others, be this within your family or with friends/peers?
- Then reflect upon how in your work setting, placement or academic studies you are striving to be outstanding.

I don't argue that as educators we should not strive to be outstanding or indeed ever drop our standards. We should aim to provide an environment that offers our young children, staff, families, and the wider community the opportunities to thrive. But what I do encourage within your reflective journey and your work is to break the mould of perfection and consider being *perfectly imperfect*.

Let me introduce you to *wabi sabi*, just one of the Japanese words that have truly influenced my thinking and approach to my life and work. The definition of *wabi sabi* is a little tricky to explain, but simplified *wabi* is best defined as the seeking and recognising of beauty, the beauty and the simplicity of life. In other words, it encourages us to detach ourselves from materialism and the material world. *Wabi* could also be considered a mindset, a mindset which witnesses us slowing down, pausing and reflecting upon the beauty that surrounds us, be this in the form of objects or humans, but all of which brings us contentment.

Sabi is possibly best defined as the passing of time and how with time things grow, change and even deteriorate. Now you may be thinking: what has this got to do with reflection and being *perfectly imperfect*? Let me explain further. As explained previously, *sabi* is the passing of time but it is also concerned with how the beauty (*wabi*) becomes more beautiful over time. Let's imagine a forest of trees heavy with leaves in the Summer, the thousands of leaves that provide us shade in the Summer. These leaves are many different shades of green, different shapes and different patterns but the deciduous trees soon lose their leaves in the Autumn, the passing of time (*sabi*). The Autumn brings change, leaves begin to change colour from green to yellow, orange and brown. As the leaves begin to fall upon the ground and time passes, they start to decay but still they provide us with beauty (*wabi*). Whilst not everyone who reads this may not agree that the brown leaves that have fallen from the tree and are now decaying on the floor are perfect leaves, the concept of *wabi-sabi* would ask us to find perfection in what is possibly imperfect.

My point is, whilst the leaves may have fallen and decayed over time their beauty remains and it is here that I wish to point out to you that, just like those leaves, we are all unique. We all possess our own unique beauty and just like those leaves we all develop as time passes. What we need to hold true to ourselves, however, is that we need not necessarily always strive for perfection all the time. We should take time to reflect upon how we can be *perfectly imperfect*.

Perfectly Imperfect and Reflection

So, what is the connection between *wabi-sabi/perfectly imperfect* and reflection? My direct answer would be, 'I'm all about *wabi-sabi* these days, especially post-Covid and perfection is so overrated.' But I only arrived at this answer after much self-reflection and this is where I invite you to begin your *perfectly imperfect* journey of reflection; it might just be what you have been waiting for.

The busy and noisy world in which we all live often leads us to compare ourselves to others, to be compliant and social media adds to this level of perfection we may strive for. *Wabi sabi* would ask us not to compare ourselves, to accept our imperfections and uniqueness.

In the world of education, we are so often measured by standards, and this can be overwhelming. Whilst I am not asking you to lower your standards, I am suggesting that not every resource we produce, every lesson we plan, and every activity must be perfect from the outset. You don't need a brand-new set of pens, for example, to begin your reflective journal. You can scribe your thoughts with any pen or pencil, even one that has been chewed at the end. This *perfectly imperfect* chewed pen says to me that the owner has been concentrating, contemplating and reflecting possibly whilst chewing the end of their pen and what is most important are the reflections that are written down.

Allow yourself to be **YOU**, give yourself time to see the beauty that surrounds you, give yourself time to reflect and, of course, work towards improvement and personal growth, but never in a bid to be *practically perfect in every way*.

Time to Reflect

Time to pause, contemplate and reflect upon the following questions:

- How many times in our world, our lives and our professional careers are we striving to be perfect, to be outstanding?
- What do you feel are the reasons for this?
- Who plays a major part in this pressure or conformity?

- As professionals, do you feel we pass on this notion or sense of perfection to others?
- Do we have enough time to stop and reflect upon the beauty that surrounds us, like our family, friends, peers, or objects?
- How can we begin to appreciate the simplicity of the beauty that surrounds us and take more time to reflect?
- How can we work with our young children in a way that celebrates their uniqueness and lets them know we are all *perfectly imperfect*?
- Are there areas of your professional practice you wish to revisit and amend having read what you have read so far? If so, what are they and how can you achieve this change?

Upon completing this reflective task, we can now begin to explore *sabi* a little further and relate this concept, the passing of time, to our own reflective practice and professional journey. This is where I actively encourage you to start appreciating, recording and journaling your reflections, your passing of time, your growth and development.

Your reflective journal will provide you with the opportunity to appreciate and recognise the beauty around you, evidencing the small wins, or even the challenges, of your day. More importantly, your reflective journal will be a record of your personal development and reflective journey. This record of reflections will capture your growth, your reflective activism and give you time to reflect upon what lies beneath you as a person, your uniqueness and appreciate your *perfectly imperfect self*. (Creative methods of reflection are covered in Chapter 5.)

Travelling along the Kawa River

Having explored what is reflection, reflective practice and *wabi-sabi*, you are now hopefully adding to your reflective vocabulary and ready to commence your reflective, academic and/or professional journey. As an FE tutor, I recall induction days and some of the first teaching sessions of the academic year where sessions were planned to 'get to know your students'. Often these came with several icebreakers. (I am not a fan of icebreakers, but that's for another day.) Then there would be your introduction to your tutor group. Very much like in Early Years, you become the key person for these young adults. It takes many sessions to really get to know your learners and I would argue that it takes even more time for learners to begin to reflect.

As previously discussed, reflection is a journey, and not always a smooth or pleasant one or one that witnesses you flourish quickly. If you begin to consider how reflection takes time, and how reflection has many twists and turns, this will help you feel less urgency about being highly reflective at the start of your academic journey.

It is my work with learners and training adults that I often began my reflective sessions with my own story, my own professional and academic disasters, retelling some quite hilarious stories of lessons that have gone dreadfully wrong. However, one thing I can say is that I have learnt many lessons from these sessions and, along with my passion for reflection, it has made me a highly reflective educator.

So, let me share with you one approach and infographic that you might wish to apply to the start and ongoing journey into reflection and your academic and/or professional journey. It all starts with the Kawa River.

What is the Kawa River?

Kawa in Japanese translates as *river* and the Kawa River has different contextual elements that represent your life. The Kawa River is the work of Michael Iwama and I believe its original purpose was for use in occupational therapy. However, within this chapter, I will be sharing with you my adaptation of the model with an infographic and description in order to support you in your self-reflection and your reflective journey. Much like its use in therapy, the Kawa River is a model of practice that aims to support clients in making their life flow better by asking clients to consider their past, present, and future. Adapting this model as a student or a practitioner will aim to support you to reflect and, much like the water in any river, find your life's energy and flow.

There are many ways to reflect, and we will cover these later in the book. I believe, however, that this model is something you might wish to use at the start of your reflective journey. More importantly, it is a model you can return to throughout your journey, in the hope you will be able to reflect upon how far you have travelled in your professional and personal journey.

As previously mentioned, every river has water and flows at different speeds, much like our everyday life. For example, think about how your river flows when you are at home after work compared to the day you may just have had at work. Does it feel different? Why is this? Is it because of the riverbed, driftwood? Let me explain this further.

So, you may now already have the image of river in your head and the water flowing, but in addition to water the Kawa River has the following elements: rocks and a riverbed or a riverbank and driftwood.

Here is a simple infographic that you may wish to copy and put in your reflective journal. Your river will flow differently on different days in different environments and at different points in your academic and professional journey, so it is worth revisiting this process at different intervals

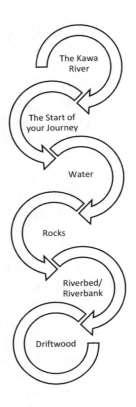

FIGURE 1.1 The Kawa River Infographic

- Water – this is the flow or life energy. In this model, just like water it is believed that life should flow and your river should be fluid and renewing. However, as we all appreciate the water in our rivers will touch rocks and the riverbank. At other times our river will not flow due to the demands of our personal or professional lives. Using this model to highlight your rocks, riverbed and driftwood will support you in visualising how you might find spaces amongst the obstructions. It is believed that the more spaces we have in our rivers, the more our life will flow.
- Rocks – these depict problems or challenging situations. The rocks can differ in size, and all may hinder the flow of the water along the river. Your rocks may be related to your current life difficulties, illness, injury, fear, concerns, your financial position, and well-being, all of which will affect your personal and/or academic and professional lives.
- Riverbed/riverbanks – these relate to environments/contexts that might create imbalance. These could be your social, physical, cultural and/or political environments which may impact upon you. For example, your social context is represented by your family members, pets, colleagues. and peers whereas the physical context could be the environment in which you live or work, such as school and college, and also much wider than this, such as the

health care system, your culture, faith, and beliefs, all of which may impact upon your Kawa River.

- Driftwood – this is represented by your personal attributes, your resources and your skills and also your values. For example, consider how your character, your personality traits, your faith, beliefs, principles, values and also your material assets and current living situation may affect the flow of your river,

Concluding, it is worth remembering everyone's representation of their river will differ, with your rocks being different shapes and sizes, and positioned at different points along your riverbed/riverbank alongside the driftwood, all of which will influence the flow of your water and life energy.

As a tutor, I have used the Kawa River at the beginning and at particular intervals in my teaching of reflective modules and in tutorials. I feel it is a model that supports self-reflection, and highlights what support you may need, as well as how far you have travelled if you revisit the model throughout your academic journey. I would encourage you to now stop and create your Kawa River and if you identify that your river is full of rocks (problems and challenges) you may then wish to reflect upon what you need to support you in your professional/academic journey and discuss this with your tutor or assessor.

Time to Reflect and Create

- Take a notebook, a pen or even some crayons/felt-tip pens if you are feeling creative.
- Using my adapted image, draw your Kawa River. Don't rush this; take time to think about your river, the rocks, the riverbed/bank, and driftwood.
- Draw and label your river, the water, and the rocks (which may be different sizes), the riverbed/bank and driftwood.
- You can keep this as a reflection and the start of your reflective journey, but I would encourage you to share your model if you feel it is appropriate so that you can gain support at the start of your journey.
- Make a note or set a reminder to revisit this model in a few weeks. Spend time reflecting upon your visual representation, make some reflective notes about the small wins and perhaps the challenges of the past few weeks. For example: have your rocks changed shape? How did you do this? Who supported you and what difference has it made to your journey and success?

The Kawa River and Teams

The Kawa River is a model which can be adapted and used as part of appraisals or as a team approach. You can use this model to identify your team's challenges/obstacles and collectively discuss how, as a team, you can each utilise your personal strengths to ensure the river flows.

Case Study

This is a case study from Dawn, a full-time lecturer in FE and HE. In this case study, she explains her professional and academic journey. As you read the case study, consider the flow and energy of Dawn's River, her riverbed, the rocks, and the driftwood as her journey in education is shared with you.

Dawn's Story

At school I was one of those students that made the teachers roll their eyes. I was always greeted with a sigh... and usually not of relief. I have many memories from school – mostly about teachers that really didn't like children. One relating to my career, and I guess self-esteem, was the careers week before taking our options. I went to the careers officer when I was in Year 3 senior school, so Year 9 in today's terms. We discussed my hopes and dreams (to become a teacher) and then the careers officer said that I was too thick to be a teacher and would never be able to achieve it. 'You have to go to university you know...' He suggested that I think of something else that is closer to my abilities... like looking after young children.

(This was in the mid-1980s – but I would argue that we are still fighting this inappropriate and incorrect narrative regarding Early Years.)

I was put in O Level classes for the first term and then moved to CSE classes because I was not able to 'succeed' in O Level and was disruptive... I was BORED!!! All being put in CSE classes meant for me was that it was easier, I did the work more quickly and I was more disruptive as I 'mucked' around with my pals at the back of the class.

I applied to college to do my NNEB (National Nursery Nurse Exam Board) – oversubscribed... I got in. I loved it and passed with the award of top Nursery Nurse. Amazing when the student is engaged. After college my life didn't offer the chance to go to university and I wouldn't have thought to try as I still had 'You're too thick to be a teacher' in my head.

When I reflect on this moment, I am often sad that I was made to think so little of myself by someone that really didn't know me. AND yet I am also grateful as the journey I took was far more colourful than the traditional Initial Teacher Training – Newly Qualified Teacher year and/or Qualified Teacher Status – then teach, teach, teach! I went into work and purposefully moved around in the available jobs to gain multiple experiences and see Early Years from differing lenses. These included – health, social services, the private and voluntary sector, and education.

Over a decade later I was persuaded to return to college to undertake my ADCE (Advanced Diploma in Childcare) by a colleague at an Early Years centre. I then completed my City and Guilds Teaching 730's 1+2 in 2001, just before the birth of my first child. Another baby and then I started to do more with outside agencies in my job role as operations manager of day nurseries – e.g: block play specialist and enabling environments for example.

I interviewed for Bachelor of Arts BA(Hons) at Kingston Uni, coming away thinking 'There is no way I will get accepted I'm not clever enough'. But I did – they offered me the place and I started the following week. After completing the BA(Hons) I undertook the EYPS (2nd cohort to go through). I achieved that and received an award for Top EYPS. I remember my BA lecturer saying, 'We'll see you again soon for your MA (Masters)' and thinking 'No I'm definitely not good enough for that'. I truly held on to the feeling of not being good enough – I now know that is an element of imposter's syndrome; however, I also attribute part of that to the constant narrative that was given to me at school.

Just as my BA lecturer had said I did return to undertake my Child-Centred Interprofessional Practice MA (ICCIP). For this graduation I took my two children. Oh, the discussions I had with their schools to be able to take them out for the day – but that's a different story!! I wanted them to put the hat on, see what it was all about and develop dreams for themselves. (PS: they have)

I am now halfway through my Doctorate in Education and lecturing full-time at a technical college and community university, leading the

BA(Hons) Early Childhood studies programme and just about to start delivering Neuroscience in the Early Years.

I worked throughout all my training, holding down a full-time job, family and all that brings alongside my education.

When I think about my journey, I know I have gathered experiences along the way that have helped me know what I do want to do. I have had some special people on the journey that have helped me believe and just that little bit of faith I guess has given me strength. Plus, I am a fighter; often if someone says I can't do something I usually find a way to 'DO IT'.

I think reflection has played a large part in journey – very much unconsciously in the earliest part of my life., However, in later years I have very consciously used reflection. Brookfield's – I talk 'lens' a lot – trying to see my situation from different perspectives and from other people's points of view. I seek others' feedback for that reason – I see the benefit of a wider perspective and, although at times it can be hard maybe even scary, I know that opening myself to the risk of other people's opinions is ultimately essential for growth. I often see Schon as I work – very in action with discussion and feedback after. I guess I could identify multiple theoretical approaches in my practice, making my reflection quite eclectic in essence.

Reflection takes time and I have chosen to carve time out for it, but I do think it is underestimated the benefits of and the time that reflection takes as well as the outcomes and or changes that occur because of truly reflecting on my work.

I find my language has changed and it now includes more reflective statements and words in everyday discussions. I wonder if this is part of my strategy to carve reflection throughout my day – essentially making it a part of my pedagogy and so giving it time and embedding it as part of my routine.

 Time to Reflect

Dawn has had an interesting and, at times, challenging academic and professional journey but has risen above many challenges and assumptions to achieve all that she has.

- Water - Can you identify within the case study where the water, the flow and the energy were at times slowed down and where it was free-flowing for Dawn?
- Rocks - What were Dawn's challenges; problems that in the Kawa River model are depicted as rocks? What hindered her progress?
- Riverbed - What environmental and contextual situations create imbalance and how do you feel they impacted upon Dawn? Could Dawn's story have played out very differently? Why?
- Driftwood - What do you feel are Dawn's personal attributes and any personal resources she may have used (or is still using) to ensure her Kawa River flows?

A Reflective Thought

For me, this model is so useful in supporting my reflections when working with others. For example, having worked with many challenging learners and in some challenging situations it has provided me with a model where I can begin to appreciate other's perspectives and try to understand that others may have rocks of various sizes set in a riverbed of environmental challenges that cause their energy and flow to ebb.

Chapter Reflection

By the end of this chapter, you should now be able to appreciate that reflection and reflective practice is a process which takes times and can be a difficult process due to the emotions and feeling it make provoke. Equally, other factors such as the demands of our role and the environments in which we work for example can prove challenging.

However, remember that reflection is personal and unique, just as you are, and being ***perfectly imperfe***ct is acceptable. What is ultimately important is that you recognise that you will develop as a reflective practitioner.

The Art of Self-Reflection

Reflection, I do believe, is an art form. It should be free-flowing, creative and personalised. Reflection should be a journey of self-discovery, a journey which includes your open and honest reflections of your professional practice. Equally, as part of your reflective practice, you may be required to write reflectively using a range of reflective approaches which you will be introduced to in this chapter.

You will be introduced to reflective theorists such as Brookfield, Schon, Gibbs and Kolb in Chapter 3 but before that let me add another new word to your vocabulary: *Hansei*.

What is *Hansei*?

Before this chapter introduces you to different approaches to reflection, I want to introduce you to *Hansei. Hansei* is defined as the art of honest self-reflection or introspection and is a combination of two smaller words: *Han* translates as to 'turn over and examine' and *Sei* is to look back upon and review the past. I have adopted *Hansei* in my own professional practice and it is here I wish to share with you that *Hansei* should not be used only when we believe things fail; it should also be used to reflect upon our achievements and successes.

Self-reflection requires time and *Hansei* asks us to use our time to self-reflect, examine, and review and recognise our wins and our challenges and to then set about considering ways to improve and create future goals for one's personal and/or professional development. This porcess involves dedicating quality time to yourself. If **Hansei** is applied as a process of deep reflection it will support you in identifying and appreciating any mistakes, errors or failures in your acadmic or vacational practice. By doing this is when you can begin to connect your thoughts and reflections and visualise them as a paper chain. Visualising a chain is useful in this art of honest self-reflection as *Hansei* would suggest that when you think of a chain you can begin to link this chain to a long chain of decisions which may not have been your best

DOI: 10.4324/b23021-2

decisions. You can then carefully reconsider each link in the chain, reviewing how you might implement a change in the chain which will, in turn, support your future development.

The Practice of *Hansei*

The practice of **Hansei** requires a series of steps. Before you read how these steps might apply to you as a student, as a professional, or even in your personal life, you can also consider how you might use **Hansei** with young children, young adults, staff members or parents.

As you read the steps of **Hansei** ask yourself: do you and can you apply some or all the steps of **Hansei** to create a reflective culture for all? How will a reflective culture or environment support you, children and young adults, staff, and the wider community with whom you may work?

In addition to the word **Hansei**, let me introduce another new word to your vocabulary. This word is **Hansei-Kai**, meaning 'reflection meeting'. You may have already experienced a range of meetings where you have formally sat and reflected, chatted, or had a formal appraisal where reflection takes place. However, the meaning of **Hansei-Kai** is much more than a one-off meeting, a single written reflection or any form of tokenism paid to reflection. **Hansei-Kai**, in this instance, can be related to the regular, in the moment, dedicated space and time for your honest self-reflections.

You may now begin to reflect further and consider how you provide space and time for **Hansei-Kai** for young children, staff members and/or parents? Is the process of reflection (**Hansei**) and the recurring reflective meeting (**Hansei-Kai**) a natural daily occurrence and an occurrence of peace and ease?

Hansei Steps

Step 1 – Find a Quiet Place to Stop, Pause, Contemplate, and Reflect

This step is something I talk about a lot in my work. The creation of this quiet space is important in supporting your reflection journey and applying the **Hansei** steps. You need to decide where this space is for you, indoors or outdoors (or both); wherever this is you need quiet time. Equally, this is something we need to strive to create for your young children and staff so that they have the time and the space to practice the art of honest self-reflection. This is the very starting point of **Hansei** as you work towards identifying ways of improving and achieving success.

Your space should give you a sense of ease and comfort.

● Consider how you can make reflection a habit, making it part fo your routine where you find the time to reflect daily.

Step 2 – Revisit and Review

At this stage *Hansei* asks you to review your mistakes. However, I prefer here to talk in terms of your challenges, mishaps, or areas where you may have been '*perfectly imperfect*' rather than mistakes. Try to view this part of *Hansei* as the dedicated time when you truly display honesty and shine a light on an aspect of your day or an incident, activity, or task where you did not achieve what you set out to achieve. *Hansei* would say this is introspection.

At this stage of contemplation and reflection, focus in on one element. Whilst this is an emotive step, it is one which gives you the opportunity to ponder, question, reflect and review. Perhaps ask yourself the following questions:

- What went wrong?
- What didn't go according to plan today?
- What was my aim?
- What did I expect?

These few questions may help prompt your reflection. However, a word of warning: please try not to make this part of the process too intense; I appreciate it is emotive, but it certainly isn't a step that is meant to leave you feeling inadequate. It is part of the process of honesty and being open and transparent with yourself and others regarding what you might need to reflect upon in your future career and/or studies.

It is at this point, if you have read any reflective theory beforehand, that you may begin to start relating this **Hansei** process to reflective theory. If you have not yet encountered any reflective theory, don't worry; you may do as you read further on in Chapter 3 where you will be introduced to several reflective theorists. No matter at which stage of your reflective journey you find yourself, I wish to remind that *Hansei* relies on honesty and truthful reflections about your strengths and areas to develop, both of which will set you on a productive path of self-discovery and change.

Step 3 – In Tune with Negativity

Being in tune with negativity comes from repeating the practice of **Hansei**. This is supported by using a reflective journal; if you don't journal already then perhaps now is the time to start. If you begin to log, note, or sketch any mishaps, challenges or, as *Hansei* would say, mistakes, it will support you to review and to seek out any recurring patterns in your professional practice.

Step 4 – Improvement and Commitment

During the final step of **Hansei**, you will need to build on Step 3. This involves not merely recognising any challenges (mistakes) you may have made, but also now committing yourself to correcting and improving your professional practice and/or academic writing.

Once again, this step needs time, dedication, and commitment. It is fair to say that in this step you may also need further support from others so that you can begin to devise a strategy for improvements. You can now begin to relate this stage to a step that, if conducted correctly, will support you breaking a bad habit. Let me expand upon this for you. I am the first to admit I love my phone and all my social media platforms; if I am honest in my **Hansei- Kai** (reflective meeting) my bad habit is that I can be distracted by my phone. This is my honest review and could stop me achieving my goals. So, my daily commitment to improve began with one small habit and that was to stop interacting with social media platforms in the evenings. In addition, I post items at the beginning of the day and if my day is a 'writing day' I place my phone on silent and put it in my desk drawer until I have achieved my target for that day.

So, here are my reflective questions for you to think about:

- What bad habit/s do you have that distract you?
- How can you overcome these habits?
- How will they help you to improve and commit?

Having now been introduced to **Hansei**, it would be beneficial to you to now stop and reflect upon all the steps once more. Perhaps re-read them and make notes as to what areas you wish to begin working on, how you can implement these stages and what you might need in terms of resources, time or support as you commence your reflective journey?

Just remember **HONESTY** is key!

Finding Your *Ikigai*: The Reason to Get Up in the Morning

It was during COVID-19 and my change of career direction and life that has most definitely changed me forever. I now had time to research and read so many unread articles, journals and books. I also began my writing career, and it was in my first book, *The Little Book of Reflective Practice*, that I introduced the concept of *Ikigai* as a tool for readers to use for reflection.

In this book, I invite you to explore **Ikigai** in much more depth and ask you to consider how you might apply **Ikigai** to your own professional or personal life, but also how you might use this with your team if you are a manager, or if you are a tutor or personal/academic coach. You can use this approach to support others in discovering their reason for being. In Chapter 4, you will also see how with a little adaption *Ikigai* has been used with pre-school children aged 3–4 years.

*Ikiga*i is a Japanese word (生き甲斐, pronounced [iki-gai]), which, like *Hansei*, comprises two roots: *iki*, meaning to live, and *gai*, meaning reason. Thus *Ikigai* can translate as 'your reason for living and being', or, in more everyday language, your reason for getting up each morning. Before, I invite you to begin to create your *Ikigai*, it is important for you to appreciate that the *Ikigai* has five pillars and ten rules.

The five pillars of the *Ikigai* are:

Pillar 1: Starting Small
Pillar 2: Releasing Yourself
Pillar 3: Harmony and Sustainability
Pillar 4: The Joy of Little Things
Pillar 5: Being in the Here and Now

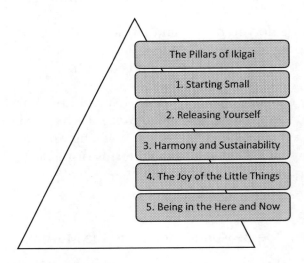

FIGURE 2.1   The five pillars of Ikigai

Before I explain further the five pillars of Ikigai, take some time to stop a while, re-read the five pillars and consider how these might relate to you as a reflective educator, as a person, as a professional and how you might use these pillars in your work with young children and/or adults. You could do this either as an individual reflective task or as a group.

Reflective Task

- Using the 5 pillars of **Ikigai,** which are:

    1. Starting Small
    2. Releasing Yourself
    3. Harmony and Sustainability
    4. The Joy of Little Things
    5. Being in the Here and Now

Discuss and define the five pillars. What do you think each one means?

How do you feel you use these pillars in your day-to-day life and in your professional and/or academic capacity?

Why do you feel each of these pillars are important in supporting you to find your reason for being?

Journal your initial thoughts and reflections. You can revisit this section after you have read more of the book and reflect upon your initial thoughts and reflections.

Explaining the Five Pillars of *Ikigai*

Following on from the reflective task, let me explain the five pillars a little further. You can add depth to your initial reflections, thoughts and ideas from the task as you are introduced to the meaning of each pillar.

1. **Starting Small**

    It really is that simple: make a start and start small. Change and your professional/academic development is a journey and so try to think small and manageable. As educators, we do this well with others, for example, we might give children an activity that is age- and stage-appropriate and allow them to be engaged more with the process than the production of an end product. However, for ourselves we might become entangled with how we MUST achieve A, B and C on our 'to do' list by the end of the day, whereas it would be more meaningful to achieve A. Basically, it is much more about the process and getting started. So, start small!

The Art of Self-Reflection

Reflective Questions:

- How do you think you could embrace this pillar in your own professional or academic journey?
- Do you stop to appreciate the small everyday wins in your life? How can you put less pressure upon yourself each day?
- What small steps can you begin to take starting tomorrow?
- How will you begin to take small steps in your professional practice? Do you fully appreciate those small steps? These small steps are your recipe for success.
- Consider the phrase that your professional development is a gentle jog, and perhaps a sprint some days. Nevertheless you cannot be marathon-ready without starting small. Every step may be small, but is significant.

2. **Releasing Yourself**

   Releasing yourself is about accepting who you are. It is about finding happiness through discovering and accepting who you are as an individual. This is a good time to remember **wabi-sabi** and being **perfectly imperfect**, but it is more to do with accepting who you are and what makes you, YOU. The use of an **Ikigai** and reflection will support you in your journey of self-discovery and acceptance. You could begin with some self-reflection:
   - Who am I?
   - What makes me, ME?
   - What are my values and beliefs?
   - What am I holding onto that I feel is having a negative impact upon my personal development?

3. **Harmony and Sustainability**

   This pillar asks you to think about your own actions and also those of others and how these might impact upon the world in which you live. Moreso now than ever before in our society, you will hear the word sustainability; it applies to each and every one of us and reminds us to be mindful of our actions and the impact these have upon the wider society and the world.
   - Can you define the terms harmony and sustainability? How do you feel they relate to you in your professional capacity?
   - How can we embed harmony into our professional practice as well as our daily lives?
   - Imagine when you meet someone and begin a conversation. How often do you stop to consider how they are feeling that day? If you are in a meeting, how often do you take on board other people's thoughts and opinions in a bid to create harmony?

4. **The Joy of Little Things**

   For this pillar, start as soon as you wake in the morning. Start to register the little things that bring you joy. As a professional, you can begin to think about your joyful practice: what specific things about your daily professional practice bring you joy? For me, it is my writing, as I waited years to freely express myself and to share my words with the world, so each day I have time to sit and write it is joyous.

   - Do you really consider the joy in the little things in life, in your studies and/or in your career?
   - What brings you joy?
   - Do you document the little things each day that have brought you joy? Perhaps you could start a joyful journal. Joy can be a smell, a sight, an activity, a feeling. The list is endless! You could practice a joyful journal in which you make a daily log of three joyful things that you appreciate.

5. **Being in the Here and Now**

   For this pillar, we can all stop for a moment and consider how fast life is and the world around us. How often are our days filled with urgency and rush. How often do we begin our days with a 'to do' list and end the day with an even longer one? This pillar of the *Ikigai* asks us to reflect upon the here and now and being present in the moment.

   - Do you have any example of how you have achieved any of these pillars as a professional, personally or within your work with young children and/or adults, your team, or parents?
   - How and what can you do to improve any of these pillars in your future professional practice?

Final Reflection

Each of the pillars of *Ikigai* are best imagined simply as pillars, a supportive structure that allows your *Ikigai* to thrive and flourish. There is also no particular order for any one of the pillars, but time spent on each one will, I hope, support you in your thinking and reflecting and help you find your *Ikigai*, your reason for being. If you look back at my diagram, you will see a triangle and the five pillars. You could copy this image and place it in your reflective journal, adding your thoughts and reflections as to how you follow the five pillars in your day-to-day life or professional practice. It may be that you feel you need to develop one or more of the five pillars and so you can begin to think how you might do this and what support you might need.

You can also revisit your reflective notes and/or your reflective journal as you travel through the rest of this chapter, adding ideas and further reflections about your reason for being and your ongoing professional practice. Most importantly, work on developing your *Ikigai*.

Ikigai and the Small Things

Just for a moment, imagine the small things you do each morning that bring you joy. For me, it's my mug of morning coffee and being greeted by my dogs every time I open the front door. These are the small things that bring me much joy. It is my appreciation of these small things in my world that bring me a sense of peace. With my coffee in one hand and my other hand fussing my dogs, I never feel rushed or anxious. It is a time where I am not being judged for my success, my value or my worth to society; instead I am relaxed, and I have **ikigai**. My dogs are just two reasons for my sense of being.

It is fair to say I am constantly developing my *Ikigai*, but I do have a mission as part of my *Ikigai* and that is to share with the education system my work, my thoughts, and reflections. I would love to see how, as a collective, we can begin to build upon the pillars of *Ikigai* and reflect upon our purpose in life. Moreover, I would like to investigate how as educators we can provide environments that take on board the ethos of the *Ikigai* for our young children, families, and the wider community.

The Ten Rules of *Ikigai*

Following on from the pillars of *Ikigai*, the *Ikigai* has ten rules. This is my interpretation of all ten rules and how they might apply to you as an individual and as an educator. I invite you to read each one and take time to reflect and apply how you might make small changes in your life to support your development and discover your reason for being, your *Ikigai*.

The ten rules are:

1. **Stay Active**
   For me, it was COVID-19 and a time of isolation that I found this rule came to the forefront of my thinking. Staying active isn't merely related to physical activity but that activity that you love doing, that activity which brings value and purpose to yourself and others. You may even see this rule referenced in other authors' work about *Ikigai* that says don't retire as opposed to stay active. I prefer the phrase stay active, as it is not age-related, but it is saying to us all, keep your mind, body, and soul alive and stay active even when your official capacity as an educator might come to an end.

2. **Take it Slow**
   Take a moment to think about how you feel when you are rushed: what happens to your thinking, your mind and body? Rush most certainly creates a level of anxiety and a sense of urgency; whilst I am not denying that there are times when things do need completing ASAP, the general rule of the *Ikigai*

is to take things slowly. This slower pace will give you the opportunity to discover new meanings, to reflect at a much deeper level and give you the opportunity to feel a sense of ease.

3. **Don't Fill Your Stomach**

The Japanese proverb of *hara hachi bun me as mantra* translates into encouraging you to only eat until you are 80% full, as this is believed to keep you healthier and help keep the doctor away. I am most certainly not medically trained or a dietician so my take on this is to consider how tired or sluggish we may feel after a heavy meal and our bellies are full. I am imagining this stops our productivity, so I am interpreting this rule to mean eat but leave a little room, so you have energy for the remainder of your working day. I would also like to think this relates to take it slow and spend time focussing on your downtime within your working day. Take time to slow down and take your break to eat and be in the moment of relaxation, all of which will hopefully prevent you from burnout.

4. **Surround Yourself with Good People**

Connecting with others is important in our academic and professional capacity and often we are judged upon our interpersonal relationship with others as part of our learning journey. As part of a team, you will meet many different characters, form numerous relationships, and connect with some more than others. Following the *Ikigai* rule, you should surround yourself with good people. I take this to mean people who give you energy, warmth, hope and joy, people who listen empathise and share your fears and worries.

5. **Get in Shape**

Thinking back to the Kawa River in Chapter 1, consider how the water in this river flows and moves. Much like water, as individuals we need to move to maintain our good health, we need to release those hormones that make us feel happy and this comes from getting into shape. Remember how you feel from a day staring at the laptop compared to a day where you may have gone outside for a walk.

Following the fifth rule of *Ikigai*, perhaps set yourself targets to move more; start today NOT tomorrow.

6. **Smile**

Concentrating on the here and now, being present in the moment and smiling is beneficial in many ways from being contagious and making others smile to showing the world you are expressing happiness. A person who is smiling shows others they are approachable and ready to communicate. Of course, there are days we don't feel like smiling or when we feel we may have nothing to smile about, but I invite you to start smiling more and see if it impacts upon your day. If it does let me know, perhaps you will be that person that fits the saying, 'they light up the room'.

7. **Reconnect with Nature**

   In Chapter 5, I encourage you to take a walk, a thinking and reflective walk as a way of reflecting. Applying the rules of the *Ikigai* try to reconnect more with nature, no matter where you live. In Early Years education, we do this seamlessly as part of our professional practice and the Early Years curriculum, we actively encourage our young children to have access to the outdoor area at all times of the day and reconnect with nature in any weather.

   As we travel through the education system, access to the outdoors becomes more timetabled and when you reach adulthood and start attending college, university or employment, you are often considered lucky if you manage to take your full lunch break to eat, let alone go outside. However, the benefits for your well-being and mental fitness are significant, so you should try to stop and go outside. Take some time to reconnect with nature, to use your senses to smell, hear and see the beauty that surrounds you. Then perhaps journal just what these were and how you feel after following this rule.

8. **Give Thanks**

   For this rule, you might wish to use your reflective diary and create a gratitude page. Following the rules of *Ikigai*, try to spend a few moments each day reflecting and giving thanks to those small things, some of these small things that others less fortunate may not have. What are you grateful for today? Write this down in your reflective diary. You can look back and begin to stockpile all your joyful moments. Do not put any pressure on yourself and make it so that you have three or four things you are grateful for that day, it can simply be one thing. Practice gratitude.

9. **Live in the Moment**

   Live in the here and the now. Live today. How often do you wake, and find that your mind begins to race? How often does your internal dialogue start racing through past events or begins to fear what you have not already lived? Following the rule of living in the moment, try to think that today is today and stop regretting the past. Make today count and fearing the future will not be conducive to your well-being.

10. **Follow Your Ikigai**

    The final rule for me is one which I feel is continuous work in process. This means that you could have more than one *Ikigai*: you can work towards a life's ambition such as gaining your qualification but still enjoy and get paid for other skills. My example for this is how much I really want my PhD and not for anyone or any institution or work, it is just my life's ambition after being told at school I would not be able to go to university due to my parents' financial status. To date, I haven't fulfilled this just yet, but as *Ikigai* is a spectrum I use my skills and attributes to drive me to share the best of myself with others. It takes time to know what your *Ikigai* is, and this takes time; thus, you should perhaps re-read this section, grab your reflective diary, and start following the pillars and the rules of the *Ikigai* on your road to self-discovery.

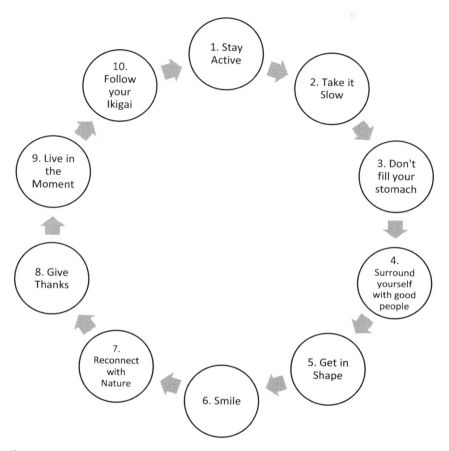

FIGURE 2.2   The ten rules of Ikigai

The Rules of Ikigai

Your Ikigai

Having been introduced to the pillars and the rules of *Ikigai*, you are now ready to begin to reflect and start the process of developing your *Ikigai*.

The *Ikigai* is essentially a Venn diagram and has four sections:

1. Passion
2. Vocation
3. Mission
4. Profession

The Art of Self-Reflection

Each of these sections has related questions:

1. What is my passion? What am I good at and what do I love?
2. What is my vocation? This may be more difficult to answer at the start of a course, but remember you should be continuously developing you **Ikigai**. So, in the here and now ask yourself what can I get paid for and what does the world need?
3. What is my mission? In this section, ask yourself how will the world, or more simply the wider community you work with, immediately benefit from this?
4. My profession. What could I get paid for?

As part of this process, you will be asking yourself questions, reflecting upon your skills and attributes and you may identify some gaps in your knowledge where you might need support, or which you wish to develop further.

Use the **Ikigai** template to start your reflective journey into your reason for being: **YOUR IKIGAI**.

FIGURE 2.3 The Ikigai Venn diagram

During COVID-19, working with the staff of Playdays, the Nursery Manager and I felt the clinical processes that had been bestowed upon us by the pandemic had impacted upon us all as professionals and we had somehow lost part of our reason for being, if you like a sense of who we were as practitioners. I decided to plan and deliver a series of online, creative sessions exploring the pillar and rules and I encouraged staff to produce their *Ikigais*. These are their *Ikigais*.

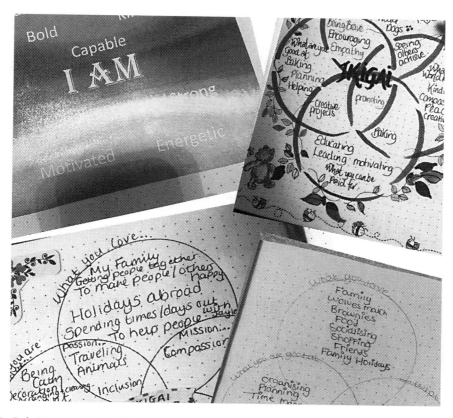

FIGURE 2.4   Early Year's practitioner's Ikigai's

Chapter Reflection

By the end of this chapter, you will now have begun to develop your *Ikigai*: your reason for being. This will support you in recognising and appreciating your skills, attributes alongside giving you time to consider your moral and ethical code of practice as you consider what the world or your setting needs as part of your *Ikigai*. By being honest in your reflection (*Hansei*), you will have spent time recognising your skills and knowledge. This will hopefully give you confidence to reflect and apply the reflective theory outlined in the next chapter to your professional practice and reflective writing.

3 Reflective Theory and Reflective Practice

The Reflective Underground

Following on from the previous chapter examining what is the nature of reflection, and having been introduced to several Japanese words, you may now be feeling you wish to adopt some of these approaches and begin to discover your sense of purpose: your reason for being. In this chapter, you can build upon this as you are introduced to reflective theory.

First, let me ask you a question: have you ever travelled on the London Underground? Whether or not you have done so, you will be aware that it is a magnificent piece of engineering. If you have travelled on it, you will appreciate the interconnectivity of the tracks, the sound of the carriage as it rattles along the tracks, often overcrowded before choosing your final destination, where you can visit the many famous sites of London.

For example, if you were on the Piccadilly Line, you would travel along this line, passing stops until you reached Hyde Park Corner where you would depart the carriage, take the escalator from the underground into the open space of London where you could then go on to visit Buckingham Palace and I believe some family that is quite famous!

So, what's this got to do with reflective theory and professional practice I hear you say? Let me explain.

In my creative and reflective mind, I view reflective theory much like the famous underground map of London. For me, reflection is the final destination station where I will arrive when I can collate all my thoughts and reflections and theory into a reflective account. Before I get to that point, however, I must travel along a few railway lines; for me, each line is a different reflective theory and each part of the journey stops at an element of the theory where I can pause, contemplate, and consider how this individual element relates to my experience and professional practice. Take, for example, the Brookfield line. As I travel along this line, I will stop at many stations which represent the key elements of Brookfield's reflective theory, such as the autobiographical (self-lens) station,

 DOI: 10.4324/b23021-3

followed by the peers' lens, the colleagues' lens and the literature lens, all stations heading towards my final reflection.

If you can imagine all these station stops are connected and part of your day-to-day professional and reflective practice, the more you connect the stations (the elements of the theory), the more reflection will take place. However, I would advise that you travel this journey many times as this will support you in revisiting your professional practice, reimagining situations and relating your experience to reflective theory.

I created the underground reflective infographic many years ago and used it for myself and my learners as a visual prompt, but it is also a useful resource for capturing your reflections in your reflective journal. You might find this useful to copy and put in your own journal.

Before you begin to travel the reflective underground, it is worth reminding you that we reflect with both our head and our hearts. For example, before you enter an experience, or set off on the underground, you play out the journey in your head. You might imagine how you will travel and arrive at your destination on time rather than how it might actually play out, which is that the first tube train to arrive is full and you must wait for a later one. Whilst you are playing this out in your head, you will simultaneously be experiencing different emotions before, during and after the journey, much like your professional practice, a lesson, or an activity you have planned. So, if you are ready to reflect, to take a journey with twists and turns, then grab your ticket and let's start our underground reflective journey!

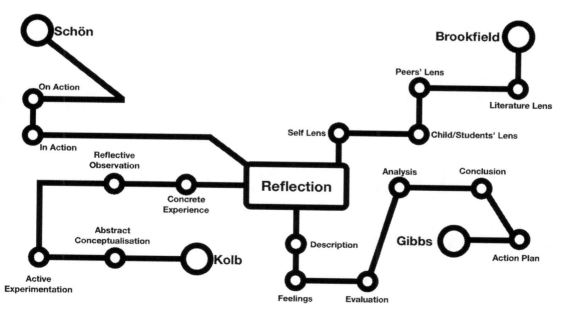

FIGURE 3.1   The Reflective Underground

Reflective Theory

Brookfield

Brookfield's reflective theory is the first one I was introduced to in the course of my teaching career. I recall being fascinated and fearful of considering others' lens in my professional practice as purported by Brookfield. I recall in my first reflective account feeling that I was more confident using my self-lens, as this somehow felt safer and less exposed to criticism. When I then had to consult with my peers and colleagues, however, it became clearer to me that I had to be more transparent and accepting of other's words of advice, feedback, or criticism in order to develop as a reflective practitioner. I can honestly say that this did take me some time to develop. I guess that what I am saying is reflection is different things to different people and that it does take time. energy and openness to begin to develop your reflections. It is therefore important that you should not feel pressured; take one step at a time and your reflections will flow.

Brookfield (1994) suggests that the more reflective an educator you are the more outstanding your professional practice will become. Whilst I feel this is partly true, I also think we need to consider the quality of the reflection we undertake, and where and what stage we are at in our reflective journey. I also believe we really need to take time to discover who we are as individuals first before we can really become truly reflective educators on the road to outstanding practice.

Brookfield's reflective theory has four lenses:

1. **Autobiographical Lens**

   The first lens is your autobiographical lens, otherwise known as your self-lens. This lens consists of your personal perspective, your experiences, and reflections of your academic or professional journey. In simple terms, it's that narrative, that story and those words you say to yourself as your day emerges.

2. **Student's Lens**

   The second lens is the child's or the student's lens (depending upon which age group you educate). Given differences in the age group you work with it can be challenging to capture this feedback. You may need to be creative in capturing these reflections. It is in this regard that I am an advocate for the reflective diary, a book, a post-it note, or a piece of paper where you can write those instant reflections to support your professional development and reflection.

3. **Peers' Lens**

   The third lens is your peers' lens, be this your fellow students, your team, or your manager. This is the one that you may try to avoid, but this feedback should be developmental and often it is intriguing to find that others see aspects of your practice of which you might be unaware.

4. **Literature Lens**

   The fourth lens is the literature lens, which is the lens where you might refer to policies, legislation, research and reading to inform your reflections. This is an ever-changing lens, as we all face continuous changes to policies, and government documents year on year. The lens refers to how these documents in the literature lens create a reflection, a need for change and also how they spark discussions that will lead you to consider how the literature informs your professional practice.

 Time to Reflect

Brookfield (1994) suggests that as a practitioner you need to reflect using all four lenses.

Using Figure 3.2, think about an aspect of your day, perhaps an activity you have undertaken, or a training event of which you may have been a part:

- What is your reflection? Use your self-lens, your autobiographical lens, to make notes and capture your reflection.
- Next consider, reflect, and perhaps make notes alongside each lens to explain how they might give you a different perspective of your professional practice.
- How will you capture these reflections? For example, if you are asking young children their thoughts and reflections, you will capture these very differently to those of your assessor or your manager, who may give you verbal feedback and/or a report, which you can then use as part of your reflective journey.

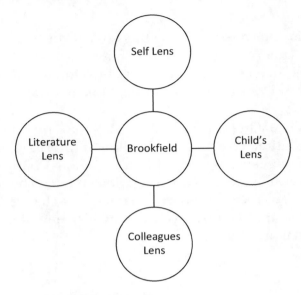

FIGURE 3.2 The Four Lenses of Brookfield's Reflective Theory

Case Study

The following story/case study will hopefully support your reflective thinking. Moreover, as you read Lisa's case study, you can consider how Brookfield's four lenses, your self-lens, the child's lens, your peers' lens and the literature lens, might be applied to Lisa's reflective account of this situation.

Our story begins with the dreaded call ... yes Ofsted would be inspecting tomorrow. Once we had all had a team brief over a few coffees we all felt braver and ready to embrace this experience, just doing what we do.

The Inspector arrived and the usual protocol took place. I was asked if we had any children with additional needs or support in the setting. I knew the Inspector would want to 'track' this child, and quite rightly, they would be observing to see that her learning needs and well-being

was being met. I enthusiastically suggested that the Inspector should join us for a sensory water play session, as our little one loved water. She had complex needs and a very rare syndrome.

The scene was set, low sensory lighting, soft fragrant bubbles in the water tray, warm towels at the ready. The inspector walked in, dutifully sitting quietly in the corner laptop at the ready for keyboard tapping observations. Our little one was splashing happily until ... she spotted the glow from the laptop. Dripping with bubbles she shot off towards the enticing glow with the promise of Peppa Pig maybe? Her keyperson jumped up behind her to steer her back to the focussed activity, but no the pull towards that glowing screen was just too much temptation! Both bubbly hands splat, splat over the keyboard with sheer joy and squeals of delight bubbles everywhere.

The bubbles were all over the inspector's suit and his very expensive looking watch ... "Disaster ... game over!" we thought, but no! The inspector burst into laughter, discreetly wiped the bubbles from his face, shut his laptop and picked up our little one and sat her on his lap!

He then started to share with us his personal background of being in SEN education for most of his career and commented on how he should have been prepared for the bubbles and that he had distracted her.

This was a reminder for us that even inspectors are human and can make mistakes, and that the promise of Peppa Pig far outweighed any beautiful sensory experience we had created.

This is a thought-provoking case study that I hope will evoke much reflection. It demonstrates how we might make assumptions of other's perspectives of us as individuals and how we may also make assumptions of others, and that we should not be fearful of using other's reflective lens.

Schon

Schon's (1983) reflective theory suggests two types of reflection: **reflection-in-action** and **reflection-on-action**.

Reflection-in-Action

To further explain Schon's term **'reflection-in action'**, stop and think about your everyday life or an event that has occurred today, and how, without even realising, you may have spent time thinking about all of it or just one part of it. You may have thought about an element of your day that has not been a particularly positive experience or you may have spent time smiling and reliving part of your day that was filled with positivity. It is important to remember that we should reflect equally upon both the positives and the negatives in our lives and professional practice as all aspects of experience give us the opportunity to reflect.

A further non-educative example of Schon's **'reflection-in action'** is when you might cook. For example, whether you follow a recipe or create a simple sandwich, both require you to follow a set of stages, such as buttering the bread before choosing a sandwich filler. It is during these stages you have your inner voice talking to you, saying things like 'This doesn't look quite right, What else do I need?' or 'Do I want cheese or egg on my sandwich?' You will then go on to think about how to either rectify a dish or create the perfect filling for your sandwich of choice. Either way, this example illustrates the simplistic nature of **'thinking on your feet'** and **'reflecting-in-action'**. Take some time to think how many times you **'reflect-in action'** in your everyday life.

Much like the recipe that may not have turned out as planned or which just needed a few tweaks before it was edible, your working day, your professional practice or your studies all require you to **'reflect-in-action'**; to make those few tweaks to an activity or change some resources in the 'here and now' before going in to **'reflect-on action'**.

Reflection-on-action

Reflection-on-action is the process whereby you look back upon the experience, perhaps an observed session, for example, and where, according to Schon, you should take time to pause, take stock and note the following:

- Identify the things that went well with the experience. Note what these were and perhaps also why you feel they were successful.
- Identify areas of improvement. Perhaps create a list of things that you feel did not go as well as you had hoped or planned.
- Analyse what happened within the experience. You could begin to reflect and note what you might do next time if you were to revisit this experience.
- List any problems such as issues with resources and/or the support you feel you may have needed to make the experience more positive, for example.
- Identify areas for personal and professional development and what support you might need.

All of these are **'reflection-in-action'** and with practice, support, and continuous reflection you will reshape your professional practice and become the reflective practitioner who reflects and shines a light on their **'reflection-in-and-on-action'**.

Gibbs' Reflective Cycle

Much of our academic and professional practice is steeped in emotions, feelings, and communication. It is how we process our feelings and reactions to a situation or an experience and how we can begin to question and reflect upon our next steps that leads us to consider adopting Gibbs' Reflective Cycle for our reflections.

Gibbs (1998) suggests there are six stages to the reflective cycle. Within each stage there is a question to prompt your reflection.

The six stages are:

1. Description
2. Feelings
3. Evaluation
4. Analysis
5. Conclusion
6. Action Plan

At this point, I would suggest it is an excellent idea to grab your reflective diary, the place where you should have scribbles, notes and/or mini-mind maps of your reflections. These notes will support you in applying the reflective theory. If you are like me, then you will often forget all the things that you do in a day. By looking back in your reflective diary you can begin to link your professional practice to theory. Also, at this point, you could begin to draw Gibbs' reflective cycle and make notes under each of the six stages. This is the start of your reflection of the experience using Gibbs' reflective cycle and will support you in the structure of a written reflective account, from which you could challenge yourself further and align Brookfield's literature lens to support the analysis and conclusion stages within your reflection, using academic literature to reference within your reflective written account.

To further explain Gibbs' six stages, here is a further explanation of each stage, along with some reflective questions:

1. **Description**
   Your description of the experience. This should describe what exactly happened; for example, what learning took place for the young children/learners,

support this information describing how the activity was planned, set up and/or undertaken and then describe what happened during the process of learning.

2. **Feelings**

   In this stage, this is where you can be open and honest and explain what you were thinking/feeling before, during and/or after the experience. For example, you could ask yourself: 'How did you feel it was going? Could there have been any improvements at the time to the activity?' It really is as simple as addressing and explaining how you were feeling and also your thought processes.

3. **Evaluation**

   During this stage, you really need to reflect upon the positives and the negatives of the experience. Try not to be too hard on yourself; sometimes when things don't go according to plan it is easy for us to feel low and only concentrate on the negatives. However, in this stage of evaluation, you need to reflect upon the negative, of course, but try to view this as the '**perfectly imperfect wabi-sabi**'.

4. **Analysis**

   For this stage, you may need more time to reflect. It is in the analysis stage that you need time to make sense of the experience. The definition of the word 'analysis' is to examine something in detail. Accordingly, to analyse reflectively you need to take your time to analyse why you feel the experience was positive or negative. It really is about trying to give as much detail as possible and look back on the other stages to gain more information to add to your analysis.

5. **Conclusion**

   At this point, you are beginning to bring your reflection to a conclusion and the simplest way to do this is to ask yourself: 'What else could I have done?' Ask yourself, at the time what else could you have done to support the children/learners? Were the resources and/or the environment appropriate? Pose some more questions to yourself and ask yourself the following: 'If you were observing this experience, what would you have done better? How could you have improved the experience in the moment and afterwards?'

6. **Action Plan**

   This then leads you to the final stage of Gibbs' reflective cycle, which is where you could ask yourself: 'If this experience or activity were to be revisited, what would you do next time? What improvements would you make?' These then are your action points.

FIGURE 3.3   Gibbs' Reflective Cycle

Kolb

Kolb's reflective theory has four stages of a reflective cycle, a model which you can use to reflect upon your experience/s and this is often referred to as 'experiential learning'. Experiential learning can be defined as the process in which you are learning through experience; thus it refers to the learning that takes place through 'doing' in your work with young children/learners. Moreover, it is learning through reflection that takes place during the 'doing'.

Kolb's four stages are:

1. Concrete Experience
    In this first stage, Kolb would suggest that you are learning from experience.
2. Reflective Observation
    Following stage one, this stage is where learning that takes place by reflecting.
3. Abstract Conceptualisation
    This is defined as learning by thinking before the final stage of the cycle.
4. Active Experimentation.
    In the final stage, your learning is defined by doing.

Reflective Theory and Reflective Practice

Let's now look at each stage in more detail and apply the four stages of Kolb's reflective cycle to your academic and/or professional practice. At this stage, you may wish to copy Kolb's reflective cycle into your reflective diary and apply each stage of the cycle to one of your experiences from this week.

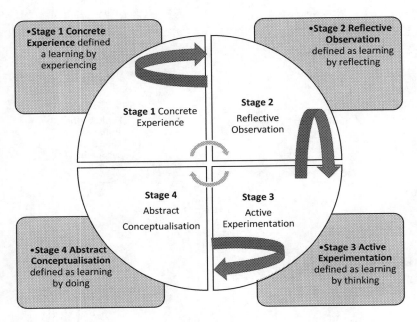

FIGURE 3.4 Kolb's Reflective Cycle

Stage 1 – Concrete Experience

This is where we can return to an earlier point in the book and one of the rules of *Ikigai*, 'living in the moment'. Using Kolb's first stage of concrete experience is much like this rule as Kolb suggests that this first stage of the reflective cycle is very much about your 'in the moment' experience. It is about recognising and reflecting upon those feelings, thoughts, and emotions you are experiencing in the situation or the activity you are present and 'in the moment' with.

You could now begin to think about one of your experiences from this week and begin to apply Kolb's first stage of concrete experience.

- Can you describe the experience? (Remember the word *Hansei* earlier in Chapter 2; this being the art of honest reflection. This is exactly what you are doing here with Kolb's theory, describing the experience honestly and developing the art of reflection.)
- Were you absorbed fully 'in the moment' within the experience? If so, how?

This part of your reflective account is a description according to Kolb; however, be mindful that in your reflective writing your tutors may wish for more detail either in this section or as you progress through Kolb's stages.

Stage 2 - Reflective Observation

Referring to **Hansei** once more, in the second stage of Kolb's reflective cycle it is once again very important to be open and honest, but this is particularly the case in this stage of reflective observation. In this stage, Kolb suggests that you begin to reflect on a much deeper level as you are beginning to reflect upon the positives and negatives of the experience.

You need to ask yourself:

- What were the positives of the experience? In other words, what worked well?
- What did not go so well and needs revisiting? Why did the experience/s play out this way?

Stage 3 – Abstract Conceptualisation

The third stage of Kolb's reflective cycle active conceptualisation is where you will begin to think much deeper about your thinking and about the reflections that took place in the reflective observation stage. Your reflective diary would be very useful to refer to at this stage, if you have not already done so.

In this stage of abstract conceptualisation, you need to reflect upon the other stages, take time to examine your writing or your notes and begin to analyse the experience. Before you begin to write analytically, try to gather as much supporting evidence from your peers, observation feedback that may have taken place, or your further reading. The use of such evidence will add depth to your reflective writing.

Once you have collated the evidence, your previous notes and/or your reflective diary, you could use the following questions as prompts for your reflections and/or reflective account.

Ask yourself:

- If I were to revisit this experience, how would I change it, the resources, the timings and/or the environment, for example. What impact might this have if you were to revisit the experience and/or the activity? It is here that any feedback you have received would be useful to support your thoughts and reflections alongside some supporting citations.

- Think and reflect more deeply about the whole experience. Consider how you might change your pedagogical approach, and why? Can you see that this stage is a much more in-depth experience?

Stage 4 – Active Experimentation

By the time you reach the final stage of Kolb's reflective cycle, you should now be able to apply the knowledge you have gained from the reflection that has taken place in the previous three stages. More importantly, you will be able to practise the new and emerging knowledge that you have gained. For example, having described, reflected, and analysed upon a previous experience, you will now be at the stage where Kolb encourages you to actively experiment and practice areas you have identified as requiring improvement. You will do this by experimenting, testing, and practising, be this a new pedagogical approach to an activity or making use of using different resources. Repeating the experience with your new knowledge will witness you returning to Stage 1 (Concrete Experience) of Kolb's reflective cycle.

Chapter Reflection

In this chapter, you have been introduced to visualising reflection as a journey. This included the infographic of an underground railway map with each theory having its key components represented as stations. Much as a train journey takes time to reach your destination, you should think of reflection in much the same way, as both a journey and a process. Whether you relate more to Brookfield and his four lenses, or Schon's reflecting-in- or -on-action and/or Gibbs' or Kolb's reflective cycles, take time to understand each theory before applying to your professional practice. Journal your thoughts and reflections daily and enjoy the reflective journey towards being an outstanding reflective educator.

4 Reflection and Research
Creating Reflective Spaces

In this chapter you will begin to consider how reflection, reflective theory and research informs your professional practice. This chapter introduces you to the Rainbow Researcher Framework, an approach which follows the colours of the rainbow – red, orange, yellow, green, blue, indigo, and violet – to guide you in how you might wish to approach research and support your professional curiosity.

The chapter aims to answer questions such as 'What is research?' and 'Why is research important for our settings and our professional practice?' Whilst this book is not a book about research as such, it is a book that offers you the opportunity to reflect and to consider how research and reflection can impact upon your professional practice.

The chapter invites you to explore a systematic approach to research using the Rainbow Researcher Framework. Whilst it is not possible to share all the elements and data from the research that took place while writing this book, you will leave this chapter with an overview of our research aim and methodology and how one reflective, creative method, the *Ikigai*, was developed and adapted as a creative research method for pre-school children aged 3–4.

Moreover, I invite you to share the thoughts and actions of the Early Years educators at Playdays, who have worked collectively upon their ethos of awe and wonder and curiosity to not only reflect upon their own professional practice but also create a bespoke, reflective and enabling environment for the children and parents – the Blossom Room. You will be able to examine the emerging results and the ripples of our research and reflect upon your own professional practice, leading you to consider how you create reflective spaces for your children, parents and staff.

DOI: 10.4324/b23021-4

Starting the Research Journey

For me personally, every research journey starts with reflection and often posing reflective questions to myself that begin with why and how:

- For example, 'Why was today's session not as engaging as it should have been? How might I do this differently next time?'
- 'How could I improve the resources?'

This is a very simplistic way to consider research, but my point is it really can be, and is, that simple to get you thinking and becoming curious about your practice. For me, I also take time to doodle, draw and note any of these thoughts and questions in my research journal. That said, I wish to share with you that I don't always research everything I note or draw, and this is for several reasons. These reasons range from time to resources. Sometimes, I find that there is a quick fix, an instant solution to my reflection,

I would also urge you to consider how much research you do every single day of your professional practice in the form of your thoughts and reflections. In your professional practice, this research possibly begins with an observation of practice or an experience which you have seen or felt and reflected upon. For me, research is also about being an agent of change and reflective activism, reflecting upon either your practice or that of your team and/or the learning environment, recognising that something needs improving, something needs investigating, and something needs researching in order to improve quality.

As a tutor, I have taught many research modules. I have often stripped back the module of its research words and begun my sessions with conversations about students' professional practice, and/or engaged in debates of wider societal issues. You will see as you travel through this chapter how all these early conversations and reflections align to the *ikigai*. However, for now let's just keep it simple and just take a few moments to think about your past week and where you may have undertaken a piece of 'in the moment' research. We can also think and reflect a little deeper and consider how one of the observations you may have made this week could lead to a future piece of action research.

 Time to Reflect

- Think about your previous week. What improvements do you feel you could make in your own professional practice and/or your working environment? Make some notes of your reflections.

- How could you make these improvements? What do you need? Who can you talk to about your ideas?
- Now consider: is this research? If you had to answer the question 'What is research?' what would your answer be?
- Do you have a research question? What is it? Share it with your peers and/or team for some feedback.

The Rainbow Researcher Framework

The Rainbow Researcher Framework was created after months of discussions with Playdays staff, being their external professional development link and commencing my own journey into research. I wanted to provide a visual stimulus for the staff, and this made me reflect upon how this framework might also offer you support for the process of your research journey. Of course, it is not exhaustive; there is so much more to research than this. However, this Research Framework does provide you with a starting point and a sequence for your approach to research.

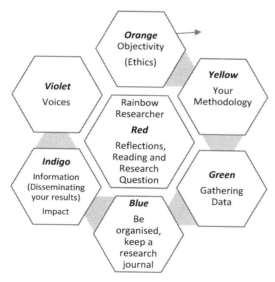

FIGURE 4.1 Rainbow Researcher Framework

How to Use the Rainbow Researcher Framework

The Rainbow Researcher Framework is a visual resource you may wish to copy and display in your setting or place in your research journal. It offers you sequential stages and a visual reminder of where to start in your research journey.

Reflection and Research

Red is for Reflections, Reading and Formulating Your Research Questions

You are now at the beginning of the research framework. During this stage, you will use your reflections and question your own practice in order to identify what you wish to research. Research is an inquiry. Therefore, in this section of the framework, you should grasp the opportunity to reflect, ask questions, and seek advice from others as you formulate a research question. Moreover, you should be undertaking further reading which will inform your research; this will support your literature review. A literature review is a piece of writing you will have to produce if you are undertaking a research module or dissertation for your studies. A literature review can be defined as a piece of academic writing which demonstrates your knowledge and understanding of the literature about your chosen topic.

Orange Is for Objectivity and Ethics

At this stage, you will discuss with your tutor or manager how to ensure you are following the ethical code of research; for example, how you will be objective, and how you will ensure no harm or distress is caused to any participants through undertaking this research. You also need to ensure you have permission to conduct the research. You will have your module specifications and tutor input for this, but as a general guide you will need to adhere to the General Data Protection Act (2016) and the British Educational Research Association: Ethical Guidelines for Educational Research (2018). This will ensure that your research proposal has ethical approval and considers issues such as confidentiality and anonymity, and how you store and dispose of the research data.

Yellow is for Your Methodology and Your Research

Choosing your methodology for your research is where you may feel your research is beginning to feel real. In its simplest form, your methodology is the 'how' of your research – how you intend to carry out your research. There are several methodologies, but a good starting point is to read further and understand the difference between qualitative and quantitative research and which might apply to your research.

Quantitative is, as the word suggests, 'quantity', meaning you will be gathering a quantity of data via numbers to prove a hypothesis. By contrast, qualitative research cannot be tested or proven, by graphs or charts, for example. In qualitative research the information and data is obtained by interviews, conversations and other methods.

Green is for Gathering *Data*

At this point, you will align your choice of methods for gathering data to your methodology. For example, if you are choosing to undertake a qualitative piece of research then your methods for gathering data will most likely be interviews, focus groups or questionnaires that elicit written responses. These methods will give you data; this will give you the opportunity to seek out the main themes or any reoccurring statements for analysis

Blue is for Being *Organised and Keeping a Research Journal*

Here you are encouraged to keep a research journal that captures your thoughts and reflections about your research. It is a phase when you can set targets and track your progress. I would advise that you note down your research aim, objectives, and research question in the first few pages as a visual reminder of your research intent.

Indigo is for Disseminating the Information. *Disseminating the* Impact *of Your Research*

After conducting your research, your findings should be disseminated. This means that you should share your findings and the impact of the research, not only with your participants but also with the wider community and/or society so that the benefits of the research are shared. It may be that your research impacts upon future policies and practice.

Violet is for Voices

This stage is very closely linked to the previous phase about disseminating the information. However, it is more about encouraging the voices within the research, including you as the researcher, to share your work at conferences, training events and more. It may be that your research impacts upon future policies and practice, meaning that your voice needs to be heard.

The Rainbow Researcher and Playdays Nursery

In my own research journey and studies, I have often had to be reminded that research is a marathon rather than a sprint, meaning that it is a slow and steady process. This slow and steady approach is exactly what the team at Playdays and I have adopted over a 12-month period. It is fair to say that prior to any research taking place the staff and I had the challenge of COVID-19 to address, along with the impact that this had upon all educational settings, staff, children, and parents. Doors were suddenly closed to parents and external visitors, including myself, and so all professional development that I provided for the team moved from face-to-face interaction to online meetings. It was during this time that the team and I looked at not only how we could be creative in our approaches to our pedagogy in such challenging times, but also how we could be creative in our reflections.

The extent of my reflective work with Playdays would possibly warrant me writing another book. However, I am going to focus and share with you how our reflections and creative approach to reflection informed our research. It was during our sessions on reflection and the use of the *Ikigai*, that the Playdays team began to develop and create their own *Ikigais*. It was whilst working with the team were developing and discussing their *Ikigais* that Lisa, the Nursery Manager and Meesha, a Senior Team Leader/Preschool Co-ordinator, had a shiny moment, a lightbulb moment or indeed a spark which planted the seed for our research.

Discussions took place over several weeks and informal and formal chats were captured and documented. We posed questions, and we were professionally curious about our practice and how it had changed during the pandemic. We discussed how the world in general, along with our professional practice, felt very different. We knew we wanted to make a change for the children, parents and practitioners of Playdays; we wanted to be led by our curiosity and so this is how we were curious and creative researchers with the use of the Rainbow Researcher Framework. This is how we created a reflective space for our young children and how this space impacted upon the children, the staff and parents.

The Rainbow Researcher Framework and Playdays Research

Using the stages of the Rainbow Researcher Framework, here is how the staff at Playdays and I used the framework to support our research and reflections of how we might create a reflective space for the young children in pre-school.

Red is for Reflections, Reading and Formulating your Research Questions

COVID-19 and the experience of the pandemic changed so much of our educational practices. For private settings such as Playdays, they remained open every day but the everyday, normal practices, like most Early Years settings, changed. One significant change was the suspension of the open-door policy for parents and external visitors, not to mention the additional measures which had to be put in place for health and safety.

Normal working practices changed, and educators had to adapt quickly; and external visitors such as myself were no longer permitted to visit. All staff were under a great deal of pressure and so we had to adapt our practice and go online with our professional development, training, and discussions. It is fair to say that during the pandemic Lisa and I also worked with the team on their own well-being and reflections. However, it was during one creative, reflective session that our research journey began. Here is how it started.

Reflections

The research began with a simple conversation with Lisa, the Nursery Manager, after one online professional development session with her staff. We were struggling to find time to work together regularly and to develop specific professional development needs due to the demands of the pandemic. However, after one session where we had looked collectively at object-orientated reflection (Chapter 5) we found a space to pause, contemplate and reflect upon our work to date. I asked Lisa the following question, 'What is your brightest thinking?'

> *Lisa's response:*
>
> *I have many sparkly thoughts; my creative brain never seems to switch off, usually in the early hours of the morning. Creative ideas and projects are very much a part of my practitioner and personal identity.*
>
> *As an Early Years Manager, I am in fortunate position to be able to implement new initiatives, themes, creative environments, and spaces. As exciting as this all sounds, I am also very conscious of the fact that others must share your dreams, visions and creative thinking – and your sparks may not always ignite.*
>
> *I reflect upon this often, and I have recognised that the sparks of creativity that I experience can be unpredictable, unruly, and often a little risky. I can now see how these ideas can be a little scary and often too much for others who need time to process new initiatives and ideas quietly. I have also come to realise that often my brightest thinking is the simplest ideas, that come from lived experiences, an emotion felt or a difficult phase or situation.*
>
> *The pandemic was the most challenging phase and time of my career; leading and guiding the team through that period was physically and emotionally exhausting. I often felt helpless in the situation, the team were at their lowest points, working in solitary bubbles, children were experiencing loss and change – how could I find a creative spark in those circumstances? I was losing my creative sparkles and thoughts.*
>
> *I started to reflect on the basics that we thrive on as humans, the basics we all need to feel valued, nurtured, loved and a sense of*

hope – what makes us sparkle? These thoughts came gently, quietly at times when I least expected, calmer clearer thoughts.

I began to implement these thoughts into practice, gentle suggestions with the team, simple ideas that were very easy to introduce without pressure or stress. The team began to spread and share these creative ideas, offering some hope to the children and parents. This was done in many simple ways, sharing sparkly twinkly lights, painted pebbles with shared messages, a mug of shared hot chocolate and a 'biccy' outside. These simple ideas provided some warmth, joy and hope at a time when it was needed most.

So, I feel my brightest thinking was my quietest thinking, a time when it was felt there was little hope to return to normality. I have reflected upon this, and I have to say these thoughts and ideas I am most proud of in my many years of practice. The simplest of ideas can have the most impact in a time of need, we don't always need magnificent sparks of creativity – just honest and humble thoughts and actions.

In response to this reflective conversation with Lisa, the two of us then decided that it would be beneficial to the staff to work with the *Ikigai* and spend some time reflecting upon the following questions within the Venn diagram that makes up the *Ikigai*. Each practitioner drew their own Venn diagram and had more than just one session to really think about themselves and begin to answer the following questions, developing their *Ikigai*, their reason for being.

They were asked to draw the Venn diagram in their reflective journals and then given no set time limit to reflect upon the following questions:

- What do you love?
- What are you good at?
- What does the world need?
- What can you get paid for?

From the Figure 2.2 earlier in the book, you will see the team's responses: their *Ikigais*. It is worth remembering that these were undertaken at a challenging time for the sector and, in particular, for those key workers who worked throughout the pandemic. This reflective time and exercise gave each practitioner time to feel at ease, to pause and to take stock of who they were as individuals and professionals.

Practitioners were encouraged to be as creative and reflective as they wished and to share their *Ikigais* verbally with their line manager, and also myself if they wished to. Some practitioners immediately loved this reflective exercise, whilst others took time to adapt and use this exercise. However, the results are astounding as the team began to think beyond their own reflections and to reflect upon how to create a reflective environment for children and parents in a challenging time.

The staff adopted other reflective approaches, some of which can be found in Chapter 5, but there were rich and reflective conversations that took place which led us to our research. The team decided they wanted to open spaces, where children could reflect upon their lived experiences, find their voices, be heard, and reconnect with their world. The team wished to use their professional curiosity to examine approaches to reflection that would give children peace and a sense of ease to communicate and reflect upon their likes, loves and worries and so we then began to ask ourselves the key question: 'Why this research was important?'

Lisa, the Nursery Manager, when asked the following questions, answered:

- Why do we need this research?
- Where has the research stemmed from?
- What's the spark?

This is probably the most poignant question that evokes so much reflection – a question that has helped me to personally process the last two years of extraordinary practice.

The opportunity and need to process those difficult years are so obvious now; however, that certainly wasn't the case when working and leading in the 'thick of it' (COVID). Being swept along by daily clinical practice, practices that seemed sterile and alien to early years, yet we adapted and accepted quickly. Parents desperately needed the service, frontline workers, key workers working so hard to keep the country moving and striving towards better days ahead. We had become a part of that effort, although we didn't recognise any of this at the time.

We cuddled, held, rocked, and soothed little ones who needed us, many whose parents were working long night shifts in COVID wards, factories, and supermarkets, exhausted and needed those cuddles and soothing themselves.

We recognised the healing and human connections that were desperately needed in our nursery, little ones experiencing loss and separation, exhausted and overwrought parents... and us clinging on to get through each day.

I knew as a leader we needed to recognise the enormity of what we were all doing, we needed to recognise our expertise and core values that make us the outstanding team that we are. It was at this point I connected with you Annie, right in the centre of the chaotic pandemic. We shared so many perspectives and reflections, Annie had created The Rainbow Educator for her first book which resonated with all our team core values. This was the beginning of our collaborative creative and reflective research.

The pandemic working became a process: we worked through, we cared and nurtured our children and families, with resilience and strength, but what we didn't anticipate was the effect it had on us as practitioners. This has become so obvious now that we are heading back to normality, it has become even more prevalent now we have time to pause and think at a slower pace.

For me, this research is needed because it has been born form the most extraordinary times, unprecedented times that we have never known before. The toughest of times that have tested the most experienced practitioner, and in doing so have evoked the deepest personal and professional reflection. Albeit the most challenging time, the 'spark', I do believe, has been created through this lived experience, honest and humble reflection, creativity and possibility thinking.

The research is needed to shine a light on the incredible resilience and creativity of Early Years' practitioners/educators who adapt and create in the most adverse situations but, more importantly, how these practitioners can use these skills to create a reflective environment for our young children. The reflective processes we have undertaken to date have enhanced our practice, given us the confidence to think differently take risks and try new initiatives with the children... that there is 'the spark'.

From this conversation we began to think of the following research questions:

- How can we create a space for children to find their shining light, their 'spark'?
- What will this space look and feel like?
- What approaches can we adopt that will ensure our children can reconnect with their world and be reflective and curious?

We then chatted further about what our research title, aim and objectives would be:

Research Title: Shining a Light on Creative and Reflective methods for Young Children in a Reflective Environment.

<u>Research Aim</u>: To create a safe, nurturing and gentle approach to engage the children in reflection.

<u>Research Objectives</u>:

- To construct and undertake a qualitative study that shines a light on our approach to capturing children's reflections creatively.
- To capture the lived experiences and reflections of our young children through creative methods.
- To develop and construct a safe and reflective environment for staff, children and parents.
- To disseminate the impact of the research project with parents and the wider community.
- To explore the implications of the study for future policy and practice in Playdays.

Red for *Reading*

In this stage, reading for any research is crucial and this is where, as a student undertaking a research module, you would begin to formulate your literature review. Equally, as a team there was a wealth of literature we had read, discussed and reflected upon that had informed our research. In this section, I will summarise the wealth of theories, approaches and thinking that we explored, and which influenced our research.

Embracing Froebel's philosophy of leading children early to reflection was the guiding principle of the Froebel approach which we aimed to achieve in our research and the creation of a reflective space. Friedrich Froebel (1782–1852), the creator of kindergartens, a pioneer in Early Years education work, reminded us how by supporting children to reflect; in turn, they would become self-aware of their own learning. Equally, the Playdays ethos of curiosity, awe and wonder aligns with Froebel, who advocates that when the children in our care are given time and space in which to be curious, creative, play and communicate then organically they will become self-reflective.

However, the impact of COVID-19 upon our young children had taken away these spaces of curiosity and self-reflection. Across the UK children were returning to Nursery having experienced lockdown and for some even bereavement, having lost family members. With this is mind, as children were returning to Nursery and a more clinical approach to practice, we began to remind ourselves of *Hygge*. Hygge is a Danish concept and the meaning of the word Hygge, I believe, derives from the word 'hugga' which means to comfort, console and which has been imported into English through the word 'hug'. Hugs were most certainly missing during the pandemic.

Reflection and Research

There are ten principles of Hygge. We explored and interpreted them to mean the following for us in our research.

1. Atmosphere – creating a space that has a calm vibe.
2. Presence – being in the moment, being present in the here and now.
3. Pleasure – life should be joyful and, in our research, we took this principle to mean how we would provide a space and activities that brought the children joy.
4. Equality – equality of opportunity.
5. Gratitude – spending time on reflecting upon what you are grateful for.
6. Comfort – feeling comfortable.
7. Harmony – playing, living and communicating with each other harmoniously.
8. Truce – removing and appreciating; there is no need for arguments. We can all express ourselves openly and honestly.
9. Togetherness – being with people who bring your warmth and happiness.
10. Shelter – a place of ease and safety.

From the ten principles, we felt that we would strive to ensure that our reflective space encapsulated **atmosphere, comfort, togetherness** and **presence** in the first instance so that children could once again feel a sense of belonging in which then to become curious again.

Intertwined with Hygge, we examined Kline's (1999) Thinking Environment and how our reflective environment would provide our children with a space to think and align to some of the ten components of the thinking environment. We took each of Kline's components and related them to our children and setting.

The ten components of Kline's Thinking Environment are:

1. Attention – listening to each other without interruption.
2. Appreciation – heightening both staff and children's awareness of appreciation. For us, we took this to be recognising, appreciating and communicating the positives.
3. Equality – each child is given equal time to think.
4. Ease – providing an environment that replaces urgency with ease for the young child.
5. Encouragement – to encourage our little ones with the courage to think but also to be mindful of being equal in our thinking.
6. Feelings – supporting our children to recognise and release their feelings.
7. Information – for us we took this as giving our children accurate information as we guided them in their reflections.

8. Difference – to prioritise diversity. Moreover, upon return to Nursery, for us we wanted to understand the different, lived experiences of our children during the pandemic.

9. Place – creating a space whereas practitioners we say to children, 'you matter'.

10. Incisive questions – in our case, we examined the meaning of an incisive question, which we believed to be a question which is crafted for the child but which removes assumptions. It is fair to say that this is the component that we felt we continually need to be mindful of and develop as educators. It prompts much self-reflection on the part of adults and practitioners and asks us to consider our own thinking, and any of our own feelings and actions that made be driven by assumptions.

From Kline's ten components we decided to focus on **ease** and **attention**.

Orange for *Objectivity* and Ethics

The origins of our research began with reflections and through the reflective and lived experiences of the practitioners at Playdays, we then began to consider and reconnect with the Rainbow Researcher Framework and the next stage being Orange for *Objectivity* and Ethics.

Working with Playdays and practitioners who were aware of their own values and beliefs, a reminder and discussion of how as a team we would approach this research objectively took place. One key point I wish to share with you is the need to consider the power imbalance that can take place within research; for example, as practitioners, it would be easy for us to take the lead in the research and so we began to think and reflect upon how our children could take the lead in the research and how we might then capture the data.

We decided that although as a team we had ideas of the research approach, we wanted to ensure we recognised the children's knowledge and experiences and so decided that whilst we wanted to adopt a creative, reflective and qualitative approach to the research we wanted children to be empowered to make decisions and so set out with a rhizomatic practice. Rhizome is a word you may be familiar with if you are a gardener; if not let me explain. Bamboo, a plant which my neighbours panted years ago in their garden; however, bamboo is a plant that is hardy and spreads. It sends out shoots, underground runners, called rhizomes, which weave, travel and pop up elsewhere in the garden. For my example, my neighbour's bamboo sends its rhizomes into my garden each year. So, if you can imagine planting a seed, perhaps a 'seed' of research. If you allow it to cultivate and propagate, it will find a new path. This is how we pictured our research with the children, since as practitioners we wanted to plant the seed but give children the opportunity to steer its direction, to be empowered and to take charge and show us as practitioner researchers what decisions we needed to make next.

Moreover, in this section any research you undertake must be ethical. You must ensure no one comes to any harm from undertaking your research and that you adhere to an ethical code of conduct. Whilst this is not a research book, you must ensure you are aware of your positionality within the research and that you are an ethical researcher who is open, transparent and reflective. If you are a student, guided by your tutor and asked to consider the General Data Protection Act (2016) and the British Educational Research Association (2018) guidelines.

In line with ethics, all permissions were granted to share the images, words and data captured from our 12-month research project.

Lisa shares her thoughts upon objectivity:

> *In my role as a leader, I am always curious. My curiosity leads me to research, fact-find and seek new knowledge. However, this research feels different; it is happening because of a lived event that we have all experienced.*
>
> *In research, we must focus on the purpose of the research and its aim. What can it tell us? How can we learn from it? How is it worthy of researching? From our reflections, it was clear that the children and staff team needed ways to reflect and tell our story. Staff needed creative way to express themselves, shake off the clinical practice, and reflect in a deeper meaningful way. Having begun this process through our own Ikigais, we then observed children who were bursting with questions and thoughts but as staff we felt that the children needed a carefully considered reflective safe space in which to communicate and reflect.*
>
> *The main aim of the research is to create a safe, nurturing and gentle approach to engage the children in reflection. We really want to hear their story, we want them to share their thoughts, and help them to make sense of such a difficult time. We aim to remain objective, as we know that some conversations may be uncomfortable, emotional for both us and the children, but we feel this is the start of a healing process, post-Covid.*

Yellow is for *Your* Methodology and *Your* Research

Relating back to my earlier words about the rhizome approach to this research, this was very much the case in this section: Yellow for YOUR methodology and

YOUR research. However, as a team we decided the YOUR research part was something we wanted to be more equal and, as mentioned earlier, we wanted the children to be the researchers and take the practitioners on a rhizomatic, research journey.

This was very much the case and the methodology and approach we were about to take became clear from one observation from Meesha, the Senior Team Leader/Preschool Co-ordinator.

Meesha reports,

> *I came into the busy pre-school room after my lunch break and I was welcomed back by 8–10 children all wanting to talk to me at the same time: 'Meesha, Meesha'. I had not seen the children so eager to speak. I couldn't listen to them as they were all speaking at the same time. I looked around and grabbed a soft toy fox. I asked the children to sit down and only talk one at a time, only holding the fox. We passed the fox around and to my surprise it worked, that's how Mr Reflective Fox started!*

As our research was still evolving, reflections from Meesha's work with the children was key. Meesha reflects.

> *I continued using Mr Reflective Fox during circle times, or just times when the children were all desperate to speak to me at the same time. I had never seen the children so enthusiastic to share their thoughts. When they held the fox, they were focussed and taking time to think. This was unusual as they usual just spoke about anything, but this was different. I was not having to lead the questioning; they were experiencing a deeper thinking process.*
>
> *I think having Mr Reflective Fox to hold and connect with has empowered the children and given them the confidence to speak about whatever they want. Quieter children are now feeling they can do it, they can speak up, you don't have to be shy and reserved, your voice matters. I also noticed that the louder, more confident children are learning to listen and tune in to other children talking.*
>
> *The children have developed a deeper thinking process, whereby before it was one-word answers, now we are hearing developed sentences.*

A further reflective conversation with Lisa, the Nursery Manager, following her observations adds to why as a team we began to choose the research methodology we did.

Reflection and Research

Lisa's words following Meesha's observation:

> *I think the research methodology and approach was always going to take a qualitative stance, using first-hand observations, captured moments, naturally occurring within our setting.*
>
> *This needs to be planned carefully with the child at the heart of each part of the methodology. Sensitive practitioners, who know the children and families, will be invaluable during the planning of each stage of the research. We could not lose sight of research title and aim to tell our story.*

Following on from our choice of methodology, we then had to consider what methods we might use, or indeed what methods the children might choose to capture the child's voice and their reflections. Meesha had already been reflecting-in-action (Schon) and used Mr Fox, but our conversations led us to recognise that we wanted a more creative outlet and a reflective space for the children. We also recognised that we wanted the children to lead and be partners in the research alongside their parents/carers.

Lisa, the Nursery Manager, and I then spoke about the sample size for the research.

Lisa noted,

> *We want to use a small focus group of six pre-school children and their families; these children have been with us full-time throughout the pandemic and are soon to transit to school. We feel that these children have so much to share; their voices need to be heard. The parents were so appreciative that we had recognised the need for this work when we share that their children would be part of a research project. Parents had shared with us how they had felt so overwhelmed with guilt at sending children into Nursery throughout the pandemic and were so thankful that we were recognising the need to offer support and for their voices to be heard in a safe and reflective space.*

And so, as a team of researchers, we had our sample size, but we very much wanted the parents to be part of the research and so, as Lisa reports,

> *We began gentle discussions with parents; they began to become comfortable, pausing and reflecting with us. Parents enjoyed this time, they discussed how this was so different to the Government focus of 'catch up pressure'. This just fuelled the guilt because of the fast pace and busy home life. These discussions empowered us, and we knew that our research was justified and relevant for the' here and now' in our setting.*

After gaining parental permission, it is worth noting a further reflection that took place. It was springtime and the Nursery blossom tree was in full bloom. Lisa and Meesha came up with the idea of a Blossom Room. They wanted to create a space that felt calm, peaceful, cool and very different to other spaces in their setting. They were not clear as to what would be in this reflective space at this point; later in the chapter, however, you will see how the Blossom Room evolved and was, and indeed still is, the space created for children to reflect and connect.

The Blossom Room

It was during the Spring that the Blossom Room became the title and theme of our new reflective space. The space that children could access to be creative, reflective, connective, quiet, peaceful, and more. In retrospect, unknowingly, I believe we were aligning our research to the very first Japanese word in this book: **Oubaitori**. If you recall, **Oubaitori** means that, just like blossom, each one of us develops and blooms at our own pace; this is exactly what we all wish for as practitioners for the young children in our care. We wish to provide our children with a space of ease and safety, supply the resources and give our professional love as we watch these young children develop from being to belonging to thriving.

Lisa records that,

> *the creation of The Blossom Room stemmed from following the children's interests. At the stage of our research where we were reflecting, devising our research focus and methodology, the children were mesmerised by the blossom falling outside. We recognised that this had a calming effect on the children. The children were calm but not quiet; they chatted about what they were seeing, and we talked about change. We then made the connection to use blossom as our safe space environment theme and focus.*

Lisa goes on to say, '**This environment was designed for creativity and curiosity. We wanted to capture that awe and wonder of the blossom falling, revisit and take the children back to that initial experience outside**'. And so the Blossom Room was created.

You really need to visit this reflective space to appreciate it fully. It is cool, it is tranquil, and it smells divine. It has gentle glows of light, lanterns, a projector for sharing images and, of course, a blossom tree where children can hang a petal after spending time in the reflective space. Playdays is not a purpose-built Nursery; it is an old Victorian house, and the Blossom Room is what I believe would have been the cellar. Inside the Blossom Room the team have provided the children with a range of choices for creativity, calm and reflection and, as you will discover, used and adapted the **Ikigai** as a method for gathering data with the pre-school children in their new reflective space: The Blossom Room

Reflection and Research

FIGURE 4.2 Blossom Room

FIGURE 4.3 Blossom Room Lanterns

FIGURE 4.4   Blossom Room Tree

As a researcher, an author and, of course, as a Nursery Nurse, when I first saw the Blossom Room, I knew that this environment was going to be an environment that the children would love. The warm glow of the room and its peacefulness felt safe, nurturing and a space for reflection.

FIGURE 4.5   Capturing reflective moments in gentle hands

Green is for *Gathering* Data

Having created a space for reflection, we then considered what research methods we would use and how we would gather data. In this section, I will share with you some of the methods we chose and some of ways the team gathered data.

Our research methods included:

- Observations
- Creativity using collage and child-initiated creative activities
- Yoga
- Reflective Fox and Circle time
- Dialogue with children, parents, and staff
- *Ikigai*

The First Visit to the Blossom Room

As previously mentioned, the children were, in part, all ready to communicate and reflect and Meesha had most certainly used Schon's reflective theory of reflecting-in-action and grabbed to hand Mr Fox so that all children could be heard at a time when they were all wishing to communicate at once.

So, as the staff recognised that the children needed more time to talk and reflect, the Blossom Room was created as their safe and reflective space. The staff wanted the children to be curious about the space and about discovering who they were, especially after the isolation of COVID. With this in mind, the staff decided to use the *Ikigai* as one of the research methods for capturing data about what the children loved, and what they were good at, and adapted part of the *Ikigai* to include their favourite spaces.

Below, you will see a snippet of the data that has been captured during our research. There are some research journal notes, dialogue captured from the children and evidence of the children's creativity as they worked on their *Ikigais* in the Blossom Room.

The First Visit to the Blossom Room

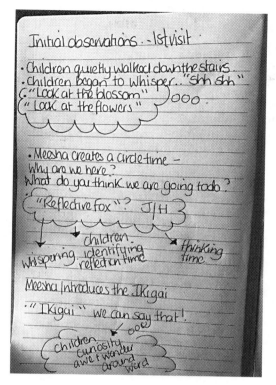

FIGURE 4.6 A Research Journal Entry

As you can see in the observation and planning section of this practitioner's research journal, the practitioner dedicated a lot of time for the children to adjust to the Blossom Room, words such as, 'shh' coupled with the children walking quietly down the stairs to the room immediately shows how the children were at ease they entered this reflective space.

During this session, the children were observed looking at, touching and smelling their new space. They moved around the room very quietly before Meesha created a Circle time and asked the children 'Why do you think we are here?' The immediate answer and reference to Mr Fox shows how the children were making connections to their previous reflective experiences. Moreover, the further responses from the children, such as 'it's thinking time', coupled with them whispering, suggests they were at ease and feeling a sense of belonging (At no point were the children asked to whisper, this is something the children did as soon as they entered the Blossom Room).

In this first session, Meesha also introduced the children to the word *Ikigai* and some repeated this back before going on to explore creative materials to begin their *Ikigai*.

Reflection and Research

Creativity, Curiosity, Ikigai and Reflection

The children's *ikigai* developed over many sessions in the Blossom Room and created as and when the children wished to, which, I must add, was during every session. Practitioners observed the children's body language relax and their voices instantly quieten; you can see this recorded in the research journal.

The dialogue from the children was captured by the staff and recorded in their research journal. The images and captions are just some of the data captured during the children's time in the Blossom room and shows them being curious, creative and reflective.

Data Captured in the Research Journal

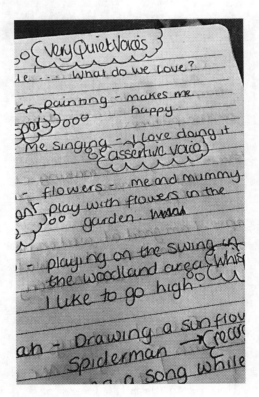

FIGURE 4.7   Practitioner's Research Journal Entries

The *ikigai* was adapted and the children began to work on the question 'What were their favourite spaces?' Using different creative materials, the children expressed their likes; whilst the team never wished for an end product from this research method, the children were so engaged during each session that they would ask for their pens, choose their materials and create.

Each image shows some of the areas of the *Ikigai* the children developed alongside their dialogue.

Whilst developing, what do you love?

One child said, **'I'm good at reading stories. I like doing this on the green beanbags. I look at the pictures.'**

FIGURE 4.8   Children's Ikigai

FIGURE 4.9   Photograph of the children's Ikigai, 'What are you good at?'

Another child reflected and answered, **'I'm good at making clay. I like to make all the patterns and paint them.'**

The children developed their *Ikigais* over the following weeks and one area of the *Ikigai* was adapted to discover what the children's favourite spaces in Nursery were. One child when asked this question replied, **'The Blossom Room is my favourite. I like to draw with the special pens in here. I can sing and draw.'**

FIGURE 4.10 Children's Ikigai, 'What are your favourite spaces?'

One final reflection from these sessions was the impact that the sessions had upon the children after their session in the Blossom Room ended. Upon returning to the other rooms in the Nursery or going for lunch, they would often ask staff when they could next go to the Blossom Room.

Blue is for *Being* Organised and Keeping a Research Journal

For our research, we knew we had to be focused and organised. As already discussed, our research stemmed from Meesha's work with Mr Fox, who has since become Mr Reflective Fox (named by the children). It was clear even before the official start of the research project that the children had a lot to say. We also knew that in our 12-month research project, we would be undertaking lots of observations, making notes, and scribing children's comments, and so each member of staff created a research journal. We also made the decision that the research journals were a space not only for data collection but also for our reflections and creativity.

What Is a Research Journal?

A research journal can take several different forms and will become very personal to you and the nature of your research. A research journal will keep you focused on the aims and objectives of your research. It is a place to keep a detailed record of your research, reading and your reflections. Moreover, your research diary will keep you organised and help you set targets for the next steps of your research and/or writing.

Your research journal can also be creative. Here is an example of the research journal that belongs to Lisa, the Nursery Manager. It shows her creative plan for the month ahead, with headings and prompts to collect data and share her vision and her reflections. This was the start of our *Being* organised in our research approach.

FIGURE 4.11 Manager's Research Journal

Indigo is for Information and Impact (Disseminating the *Information and Impact* of Your Research)

In any research project, the results, along with the impact of the research, should be shared with your research participants. As we developed different methods for capturing data within the Blossom Room, the Nursery staff displayed how the children were being active researchers and how the research methods were forming an integral part of the Early Years curriculum and Playdays planning.

The Parent Information Board

FIGURE 4.12   Photograph of Parent Information Board outside Nursery

Below is a sample of Playday's planning, where you can see how reflection, the *Ikigai*, Mr Fox, Yoga, creative activities, and more form part of the research project and gave us all the opportunity to gather data. Moreover, I invite you to revisit the pillars of the *Ikigai* (Chapter 1) and using Playdays' planning note where the children are given the opportunity to follow the five pillars of the *Ikigai*:

1. Starting Small
2. Releasing Yourself
3. Harmony and Sustainability
4. The Joy of the Little Things
5. Being in the Here and Now

This example of one week's planning was shared with the parents.

Playdays Planning

Area of Learning	Activities	Key Vocabulary and Questions	Children's Learning and Interests	Ways to Further Develop Learning
Communication and Language	Daily circle time discussions. Creating a reflective Ikigai in our blossom room Focus on the letter b for butterfly	Reflections with Mr Fox Group reflections and discussions surrounding our favourite things to do at nursery, people who are special to us, our favourite places, things we are good at doing.	Focus on the end of the hungry caterpillar story, discussions about change and transformation. Using our photographs that the children have taken as a discussion starting point.	Ask your child about their favourite spaces/places and why?
Personal, Social and Emotional Development	Trapeze rope swing and the tree swing. Mirror play outside, using the large, curved mirror. Working together to make a giant butterfly.	Helping each other, pushing, turn taking. Developing a sense of self, our bodies. Recognising ourselves, our features, developing a sense of self. Choosing and selecting resources together, sharing glue sticks, scissors, allowing others to contribute.	Learning to share, turn take and play co-operatively. The children are interested in each other now, differences, similarities, likes and dislikes. The children are developing co-operative skills, negotiating, and valuing each other's ideas.	Can you find a place to climb and swing? Share any photos with us! Can you make a beautiful butterfly?

Physical Development	Yoga stretching sessions Clay work	Discussions around physical movements, stretch, push, reach, turn, bend. Developing hand muscles manipulating the clay, push, poke, stretch, pull, flatten.	The children are discovering different physical movements and how their body can work in different ways. The children are developing dexterity and are using all the little muscles in their hands and busy fingers.	Try some moves at home.
Literacy	Story time sessions Focus on writing the letter b on various surfaces Blossom room experiences	Using large surfaces, outdoors, tabletops, chalk boards to experience 'writing'. 'writing' - mark making in our ikigai circles together.	The children are developing the skills for letter writing, providing large areas to develop the formation of letters. The group are enjoying experiences where they can experiment with writing.	Provide opportunities for writing skills, tabletops, trays, in bubbles, water and a paint brush on patio slabs outdoors. Can you spot a blossom tree?

Area of Learning	Activities	Key Vocabulary and Questions	Children's Learning and Interests	Ways to Further Develop Learning
Mathematics	Symmetrical patterns	Looking at symmetry using the butterfly theme this week. Encouraging the children to recreate their own symmetrical patterns using the mirrors in the blossom room.	The children are noticing patterns in materials, nature, block play and construction	How many patterns can you find at home?
Understanding the World	Focus on the life cycle of a butterfly Looking closely at the blossom trees	Extending language around the natural world. Discussions the structure of the tree, the branches, and the blossom flower. Watching the blossom in the wind in the nursery garden.	An interest in springtime has developed through outdoor play. The sound of the birds, the new growth and the blossom falling.	
Expressive Arts and Design.	Creating our ikigai, allowing the children time and space to be creative. Creative experiences in the blossom room, using multimedia.	Using the blossom room space to inspire the children, a reflective space to be creative. Using the soft pink lighting and light box to inspire the children to create their own representations and drawings.	The children are enjoying and being motivated by the quieter reflective times together. They are choosing ways to create The studio area is a beautiful space to enhance our creative experiences.	Talk about our ikigai reflective work.

Note: This weekly plan was based on the children's current interests at the time; it does evolve and changes with the children's thinking and motivation.

The Emerging Results

As our research data was collated there were some clear emerging themes that became evident from the creation of the Blossom Room.

As a team, Playdays had created a safe, nurturing and gentle approach to engage the children in reflection in the shape of a Blossom Room: the research aim. This space had elements of **Hygge**, atmosphere, comfort, togetherness and presence in addition to Kline's components of ease and attention.

With ease and attention, the qualitative methodology and range of creative methods were implemented, including the use of the **Ikigai** to capture the children's lived experiences and reflections. The team observed children who began to feel ease, and were relaxed, curious and creative in their reflections (Froebel).

The children had received the opportunity and time to think, to talk, to be peaceful and to reflect and connect with their environment. Moreover, we observed children who were curious to discover their likes, and loves; their **Ikigai**.

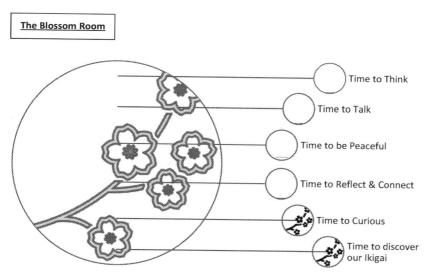

FIGURE 4.13   Emerging Themes

Violet is for *Voices*

You might think that in our research we had captured all the voices we needed in our data and indeed we had; we had disseminated our research findings with staff and parents/carers. However, in terms of the Rainbow Researcher Framework 'voices' refers to how we can raise our voices as a collective to support our professional practice and our reflections and to inform the future policy and practice within our settings and/or the wider community:

What are the next steps in our reflective journey?
What voices do we still need to capture after the research?
Who can we ask to give us their open and honest reflection?

Through staff conversations, it was clear the ripples of the research had rippled through the other practitioners' rooms with children of different ages. Moreover, as restrictions eased post-pandemic, and the Nursery doors were beginning to open now to parents and visitors we had parents wishing to visit the Blossom Room. We wanted to capture their voices.

Voices – Opening the Doors of the Blossom Room to Parents/Carers

Upon completion of the children's *Ikigai*, small groups of two children, accompanied by their parents/carers, were invited into the Blossom room. There was no set agenda; the children led the session, showing their parents the space and, of course, they chose to be creative and curious. The staff involved with the research project were present and as this space offers ease and comfort, one parent openly spoke about the impact of the Blossom Room.
    We captured their voice:

> *I've definitely seen the benefit of the Blossom Room and the reflective sessions for my child. Over the last few months or so, he has really learnt how to focus, express himself even more so than before and find the benefit of every task he does. He's always been very high energy, but he's really impressed me with the way he articulates himself.*
>
> *Reflection is definitely something I endorse. Reflective Mr. Fox (great idea Meesha!) has really enhanced the way my child communicates and expresses himself. So many children don't talk about their feelings or will go through things and won't tell anyone or won't know how to express themselves. Jesaiah has always been one to talk but he really thinks about how he feels and how that affects him; he will even come up with solutions! His independent thought process is quite mature given he is only 4 years old. For example, when he's tired, he will take the time to evaluate whether he should play or rest. The first time I heard him say, 'Mommy, I'm tired, so I think I should go to bed', I was in disbelief!*
>
> *Even from a confidence perspective, Meesha has told me of so many 'fears' he's overcome - like the wobbly ladder in the garden! He was so proud of himself when he finally conquered it!*

What's really pivotal for me though, is Jesaiah's focus. He used to only want to play superheroes with his friends (because he's Miles Morales after all). He wouldn't be interested in any other activity and would rush to complete it so he could be Spider-Man! However, the blossom room has really flicked a switch. Jesaiah wants to take part in other activities, realising that he needs to take part because it's beneficial to him but knowing that there's a time and place to play superheroes and he won't be missing out by doing something different. What's amazing is, when he is in the zone, he will sing his favourite songs from the Spider-Man: Into the Spider-Verse *soundtrack – evidenced by the beautiful recording Meesha and Lisa shared with me! So, Spider-Man still plays a part in his focus and creativity. He's so determined to get things right, but also learning patience. I've seen that especially when practicing writing his letters. He will keep trying until he gets it right, because he knows he will get it right eventually and he knows how good it feels when he does.*

To conclude, I think Jesaiah has benefited tremendously from reflective therapy. The earlier children can learn to express their feelings and be encouraged to be their true selves, the more confident, focussed, expressive and open they will be. We will be building the perfect foundation for our children as they tackle this big scary world!

This was an overwhelming reflection and aligns to our research objective: to develop a safe environment for parents/carers in addition to children and staff. I was fortunate to be present in this session listening to this reflection. However, the voices continued and, later that day, Sarah, the Deputy Manager and Baby Room Leader, reflected,

I just think that the children returned to new nursery life that was so different for them. They had been gone for such a long time and then suddenly found themselves back again.

I felt so anxious, constantly asking myself, how can I claw back all the lost social interactions together, how can I bring them back closer together in these circumstances?

If I talked to anyone at home they didn't understand, it was hard to switch off, doing the best for the children was always in the back of my mind, but how?

I felt I needed to find myself again as a practitioner, I felt useless, I couldn't care for the children in the way that I was used to.

Annie came along and through reflective sessions showed us how to value ourselves, trust our knowledge and remember who we were.

The research had to happen to make recognise a unique situation, the children had lived through it, it couldn't be ignored.

Reflection and Research

Sarah is now accessing the Blossom Room with the babies and was last seen with the light box and feathers and some very curious and reflective babies.

Departing and Transition

By the end of our research the pre-school children were ready to leave Playdays and transition to their next adventure. The theme of the Blossom Room goes with them in the shape of a blossom stone created by Lisa, the Nursery Manager, and the message that is passed to each child reads. **'Always remember what you are good at, what you love and always take time to have a little think.'**

FIGURE 4.14 Hand painted stone of transition

Chapter Reflection

I can honestly say that I never imagined that the research for this book would evolve as it did. I underestimated the impact the research would have upon practitioners, children, staff and myself. As a reader, I hope you are inspired to reflect upon the environments you provide for your young children, and that you grasp the opportunity to use the Rainbow Researcher Framework to support you in approaching research that will hopefully lead to the creation of a reflective space for the young children in your care.

5 Creative Methods of Reflection and our Reflective Space

Creative Ways to Reflect

At this point in the book, you will have read my references to a reflective journal and read how I actively encourage you to keep one of your own. However, there are several ways to reflect and I for one enjoy a creative approach to my self-reflection. In this chapter, you will be introduced to several ways to capture your reflections. You will explore how you can capture your reflections in a much more creative way.

As a tutor, I have often complied with modules of study and my students have dutifully completed written reflective accounts, both on paper and online. However, as my appreciation and passion for reflection has grown so has my understanding and knowledge of how we can approach reflection creatively. I also believe that as individuals, we must take time for pre-reflection; by this I mean taking time to reflect upon who we are as a person before we begin to reflect our professional and/or academic identity. I believe that once we have taken time to reflect upon ourselves, our attributes and/or our values and beliefs, we can then spend time reflecting upon how these might impact and support us as professionals. In this chapter, you will be able to share some examples of individual and professional creative reflections from educators who have worked with me face to face and online. Their reflections and creativity will hopefully encourage you to begin to become more creative in your approach to reflection.

DOI: 10.4324/b23021-5

Creative Methods of Reflection and our Reflective Space

These approaches include:

1.STOP	2.SNAP	3.POST IT	4.THINK & SHARE
Take time to stop. Pause, contemplate & reflect upon your day	Take pictures of the day's events. SNAP the wins and the challenges.	Capture your reflections on post it notes.	Reflect and share with a reflective buddy.
5.OBSERVE	**6.READ**	**7.DRAW IT**	**8.WALK**
Take time to stop and look around you. Observe the room.	Read, Research and Reflect.	No artistic license needed simply doodle your reflection.	Take a reflective walk. Take in the power of green.
9.JOURNAL	**10.ASK**	**11.REFLECT &CONNECT**	**12.OBJECTS**
Keep a Reflective Journal.	Ask others their thoughts, use their lens for reflection.	Interact on social media capturing reflections.	Gather objects that represent a reflection of your day.

FIGURE 5.1 Ways to Reflect

1. **Stop**

   Quite simply, you need to STOP before any reflection can take place. Find a space in your day to pause, contemplate and reflect. No creativity or reflection can possibly take place if you are stressed or feeling a sense of urgency. Make reflection a habit.

2. **Snap – take pictures of the day's events. SNAP the wins and the challenges**. Obviously, this approach must meet with the General Data Protection and Act and Safeguarding if you are considering capturing your working day. Snap, for me, is not about taking photos of your workplace; it is more about creating a collage of images or pictures from magazines, for example, that can be used to produce a collage of your self-reflection. Let me give you an example. I once made a collage of hats – all shapes, and sizes – and I presented this to my tutor as a reflection of my week in teacher training. I sat with my tutor and reflected upon how overwhelmed I was by the different hats I had had to wear in my very first week on my PGCE. Organically, I was able to link this to Brookfield's autobiographical lens and my first reflective account was uploaded to my shared space with my tutor as a collage.

3. **Post-it – Capture your reflections on post-it notes**.

   This really needs very little explanation. I am fairly certain I have yet to encounter a single educator who doesn't have a set of post-it notes. These days they come in all shapes and sizes. They can be used as a way of record-ing one-word reflections and popping them in your reflective diary to revisit or perhaps used for whole-team daily or weekly reflections. At this point, if you are using this method to reflect as a team, it is worth remembering that whilst some individuals will openly reflect and add their reflections to post-it notes, not all of us are comfortable with sharing every single reflec-tion. Thus, there may need to be an additional reflective conversation with these individuals.

4. **Think and Share – Reflect and share with a reflective buddy**
   Many of the creative ways to reflect thus far have been self-reflection, some-what private and personal reflections. Why not try a more courageous way by reflecting with one or more fellow practitioner? This could involve reflecting and sharing face to face with an audience, be this your tutor, your assessor, or your peer. Try not to rush this reflection; take time to all sit quietly first and think, then give each other time and space to share your reflections.

5. **Observe – Take time to stop and look around you. Observe the room**.
   This approach once more requires time. Ask yourself how often you stop a task and really observe the room, the environment you are in. Take time to reflect-in-action (Schon) as to what is happening. Moreover, when you do this, how do you capture these reflections? Let me give you an example. As a lec-turer, I know how rushed I can feel to deliver a lesson, to gain feedback. This was a similar experience when I was a Nursery Nurse. There is always some-thing or someone requiring your attention and so often we don't stop, and we don't record our observations. To overcome this creatively in my teaching sessions, I often keep a piece of paper by me. On this I can either doodle an image or write down a word. I have even been known to ask my learners to shout back a word to me at the end of the lesson to help me remember my reflection-in-action. I can then use these observational reflections to inform my professional practice; this may involve, for example, changing a lesson format, or reflecting upon an element I enjoyed and wished to revisit. It also involves being honest and reflecting upon and noting down the challenges.

6. **Read – Read, Research and Reflect**
   In any academic or professional development journey, you will be required to read. This is your research. What you do with this new acquired infor-mation is when you need to reflect. You might ask yourself: How has this literature changed, challenged, or supported my thinking? I also want you to consider how other literature, including material not necessarily related to your studies, informs your reflections. I can give you an example here of a book I have sat on my shelf in my home office. This book is *The Secret Garden* by Frances Hodgson Burnett. I must admit that as a child, I wasn't particularly interested in this book. However, I came across it a few years ago while cleaning out my home and I re-read it. I began to imagine and reflect

on the secret garden within this book, a garden whose beauty has been hidden away for years, until it was discovered by the two small children in the book, was very much like my classroom research. What I mean by this is that I would often enter my classroom and begin an action research project of my own – anything from researching how my learners reacted to creative plenaries to whether or not a new set of chalk board pens would ignite energy in the classroom.

However, the point of this observation is that no one would ever ask me about my research, I never shared my research, and so I believed my research was trapped within a secret garden. This insight prompted me to invite others to be part of my classroom teaching, to post ideas on social media and more. The point I am making is that your reflections can stem from all kinds of literature – all you have to do is READ!

7. **Draw it**.

For this, no creative skills are needed. I believe that perhaps when we are rushed, doodling an image and/or drawing if you so wish is not only a great reflective tool but also a way to be mindful and 'in the moment' with the reflection of your day. I often sketch my reflections; on other occasions I doodle or create an elaborate mind map. Either way it's reflective.

8. **Walk – Take a reflective walk; Take in the power of green**.

There is a wealth of research that supports the benefits of us being outside. Taking in the power of green and walking in an open space and even taking time to look up means at least we have taken the time to STOP. After all, we don't all live in the countryside but even our cities can give us that sense of peace and connection! Moreover, it can either give you or restore a sense of calm and encourage you to be reflective as you dedicate this time to being peaceful. I recall working in the city centre of Birmingham and walking to my car or for the train most days with my head down and on a mission. I rarely looked up. However, during an induction day, a senior member of the teaching team took us newbies on a walk of the city and made us stop frequently and look up. What I saw and now see is a city filled with architecture, pattern and shape. It fills my head with thoughts of who works up there, who lived there, the year in which this was created. Most importantly, it makes me stop,

In our busy lives and in a world of rushing around, setting aside time to walk and/or go outside can be one of the most challenging things in this list of creative ways to reflect to achieve. However, I urge you to try.

9. **Journal – Keep a Reflective Journal**

Keeping your reflections in one place is something I highly recommend. This can be in the form of an electronic journal, a handwritten journal, or a mixture of both. A reflective journal is a space where you can make daily or weekly entries in a way that suits you, be this in words or images. It is a space to log all the positives and the challenges of your academic and/or professional journey. It also allows you to look back and reflect upon how far you have travelled in your studies and professional practice.

In your reflective journal, you can write in the first person and your journal pages organised as you wish. For example, my reflective journal is more like a scrap book some days; it has washi tape, images, mind maps and the odd photo. As you begin to keep a reflective journal, don't worry too much about linking your reflections to theory, as this will come in time. The most important thing is to face any fear you may have of being reflective, being creative and/or writing in that first person and just have a go. Get going!

Try not to mistake a reflective journal for a bullet journal, which can contain tasks and lists. Your reflective journal is not the space for this; your reflective journal is for identifying and recording your thoughts, feelings, emotions and reflections. You can further enhance your journal as you progress with your course and/or your professional development. For example, you can use this space to begin to identify areas of your professional practice that need development which will lead you to critically analysing and evaluating how you might make this change, reflecting-in and -on-action (Schon).

Your journal is also a space where you can add reading and literature that has inspired you, links you can make to reflective theory and possibly action points for the future.

10. **Ask**

I don't mind admitting I have improved tremendously in this area of reflection. I believe this is after all my work on reflection and appreciating **wabi-sabi, perfectly imperfect**. By this I mean that I have come to appreciate the support and guidance that surrounds us, that is waiting to help you, and by asking others their thoughts and reflections. This will inform your academic, professional and personal development. Moreover, asking others and how you capture other reflections can also be creative. For example, your tutor might give you a post-it note with one word on or your students/children might doodle their reflections. Whichever way others support you in their reflections will have a positive impact upon you and sometimes all we have to do is ASK!

11. **Reflect and Connect – Interact on social media #ReflectConnect**

Social media can prompt you to reflect and connect with others. Take time to set up a Twitter or LinkedIn account and begin to follow accounts that are educative, positive and reflective. Often a quote, an article or a thread will prompt you to be reflective, to accept or challenge a viewpoint professionally. Reflecting and connecting with others will support you in networking as well as reaching out for support. Why not join me in my #ReflectConnect space on social media?

12. **<u>Objects – Gather objects that represent a reflection of your day</u>**.

My fascination with reflection and objects stems from my time teaching 16–18-year-olds reflection and reflective practice. Using my observation skills to reflect, I would often observe the room, this being my teaching space, and see some learners puzzled by reflective theory. Reflecting-on-action (Schon) and using my student's lens (Brookfield) I recall asking my students what they were finding challenging. I listened to responses like, 'I just don't get it', and 'I don't really know who I am'. Reacting to these comments, I decided to re-examine the module. I was very courageous and I removed all the Power Points, all the reflective theory literature and spent time simply sitting with the students encouraging them to be simply begin to appreciate who they were as individuals. I asked all my students to begin to gather objects which they felt best represented them as a professional and to be able to explain their choices. This was the beginning of their reflections as to who they felt they were as an Early Years practitioner. The students were given the choice to share with me as their tutor, with a peer or with the whole group.

Objects were added each week as the students reflected upon themselves and we then moved on gathering objects that represented them as practitioners. I observed students grow in confidence, their 'speech' became reflective and the synergy between theory and practice grew.

Reflective theory was re-introduced after a few sessions and I invited my students to then add objects to their collection which they felt others would add for them, for example, 'What might their assessor add as an object from a previous observation?' In this instance, I recall one student adding a ball of string, stating that this object would be an object her assessor would add, as she had stated that as a student practitioner, she had observed how she was making connections between her academic studies and her work on placement. She also reported that the string was representative of how she was 'unwinding and unravelling'; by this, the student meant she was becoming more confident in her abilities, and she could see how she too was making those connections in her professional and academic development.

I have since used this method of reflection in many of my sessions and here is an example of how one professional has used object reflection. Jessica Max is a Headteacher, and SENCO (Special Educational Needs Co-ordinator) and she has openly shared her self-reflections using objects. Jessica and I have worked online together using object reflection. After my session she was given time to think, collect and reflect. This is her response:

In some way or another, all these items interconnect and interweave with one another which I'm hoping will become clear…

Where to start:

The bucket – the bucket is a bit like my version of a Mary Poppins bag. Professionally, I use it as part of the attention autism programme to help the children with Autism Spectrum Disorder with their focus and attention, hopefully leading to spontaneous and in-context speech. It is quick and exciting. I always have new things in my bucket or for my bucket and have actually been called Mary Poppins. The programme, I feel, works for all children regardless of a diagnosis; therefore, at some stage or another, all the children in the nursery will participate in my bucket time and the next stages. From a personal perspective, my own daughters loooooove the bucket and requested I do it at home too. I often find them pretending one is me;, the other watching and vice versa. I love sourcing materials for inside my 'Mary Poppins' bucket but the real reward is knowing that most of the children are ready for the next stage which means it's working. Plus, the joy and focus each time I bring out an item is magical.

Books – I am a bookaholic and have been since a child. You may have spotted your book in the little pile... just received and looking forward to starting it! Books, for me, have been an escape. Doesn't need to be fiction. I have a passion for learning and believe that life is one great learning journey. Apparently as a child I often worried my parents when they couldn't find me as I'd be tucked away in a little corner, usually behind a door, reading a book. At work I am encouraging a love for books and make sure there are books in every area of the room. We also send books home on a weekly basis. Some children choose the book they want to take; others aren't there yet so I carefully select a book that fits in with their interests and gradually branch out to try to extend their interests. At home we have a gazillion books. I will never forget when one of my friends told me I was mad – mad for lying on my bed with a new-born baby reading her stories. 'It's not like she will gain anything or understand the story.' I was told... but hey ho, at around 6 months old she was making it very clear which book was her favourite and I have two very avid readers at home; one who loves her fiction and picture books, the other who loves her facts and will sit for hours reading an encyclopaedia or dictionary!

Notebooks and pens – I have an abundance of these as do my children. The wackier the better! I always carry a notebook and pen with me and have one by my bed for those 3 a.m. moments that I don't want to forget.

Crystals – strong and powerful, super soft and super hard, smooth, and spiky. Crystals came into my life due to illness as a teenager and

I fell in love with them and with the idea of each one being so unique, individual, and resonating at different energy vibrations that connect to the body. They take me into the marvel of the natural world and Mother Nature at one of her finest. They saw me through a hard time and created an interest that wasn't just about the healing element but also the geological and aesthetic. I had a phenomenal collection but was convinced by my ex-husband that they were no longer 'needed' as a part of my life and therefore I sold most of the collection to pay off his debts and help when he lost his job. At the time it felt right but I didn't know he was going to be my ex then either. In some respects, there's an element of bittersweet as they came into my life through illness, left my life and gradually they are wending their way back into my life (partly through illness). I never stopped loving them; I have kicked myself numerous times for selling most of them. However, my daughters are showing an interest in them, and I am acquiring more again as illness struck me again. Covid hit me very hard and once I managed to get the breathing under control (ish) I could feel my body taking me right back to my teenage years of illness and taking me right back to searching for alternatives to help make me feel better. In some respects, I feel like I've gone backwards in my life as a result, but in other respects it's different and bringing back or re-awakening something that needed to be there. Long Covid is a killer!

Music – music is everywhere. Music is a massive part of who I am. Music was my life and still is but in a variety of different ways. I grew up in a musical family with a professional musician for a mother. But it is more than that... music is powerful; it's a form of communication like no other, it reaches us in ways that are inexplicable yet so utterly moving. Here you see samples of many CDs I have, a lot of them my mother's and I helped her get there. (I can explain more if you want/ need.) I dreamt of being a world-renowned flautist but deep down knew I didn't really have it in me. I dreamt of being a music therapist but my body had other ideas. Nevertheless, music is a massive part of my life and got me to where I am now. Had I not started my own music and movement sessions and managed to convince my daughter's nursery to take my sessions, where I combined the music and movement with story time and puppets, I'd never have gone on to qualify with the Early Years Teacher Status and work my way up to the position I'm in now. Every day is musical; my own daughters were singing and dancing before walking and talking. Alexa is on all the time and my daughter is now learning piano as well. Our life is one great big musical and always will be. The children at nursery have music every day and I bought them an Alexa too! They love it. At home and in nursery we always have an assortment of instruments available. It's noisy, but it's music! Having lost my mother six years ago I struggled with listening to music but its power is immense and I will never lose that.

This brings me to the hands. One was my mum's, and she gave me the other. Hands were her essence and her music. Hands are everything. When I am teaching the children hands are not for hitting etc. I ask them 'What can we do with our hands?'... the list is endless and powerful just like music, just like reading, just like writing... Through our hands we absorb, we are creative, we are nurturing and caring, we are so many wonderful things.

Jewellery – like you said, you can't teach without your lipstick on. I feel naked without my jewellery. The majority of my jewellery was either given to me by my mother or belonged to her which I inherited. I have jewellery made and bought by my daughters and by the children at nursery. I've put here just a small selection of very meaningful pieces, including handprints of both my daughters and my mum. My jewellery is significant and has a lot of sentimental value to me. I feel naked without it and am so touched by having received all sorts of jewellery items from parents/children at nursery who have clearly picked up on my jewellery wearing lol.

The rainbow jar – made during lockdown. A reminder to ourselves and loved ones that there is love, light and colour even in the dark times. In the jar we put our wishes, sometimes a candle and more often than not a crystal. This is my home version made with my girls when I was fighting for my life, but we did this in nursery too and the children loved their little 'jars of happiness'.

Tortoise – one of our pets. Meet Speedy Poptart. He is a male 6-month-old who drives our cats insane, although the Guinea pigs are now doing a good job of that too. We love animals. We love nature. We love caring and protecting our animals. All of our animals are adopted. We have now also joined a club where you can track various animals on an app, so we are tracking elephants, polar bears, a shark, turtles and penguins! We have adopted hedgehogs, foxes, a panda and a dolphin... in the nursery we are teaching them that everything needs to be looked after and cared for, both living and non-living. We have fish and chicks and I have created a pond so we should be getting frogs soonish (tadpoles are in there). The children are learning about growth and decay and what we need to do to help our environment *and each other. We have talked about not wasting food and will be sponsoring a child; we have talked about not throwing litter on the floor/ground so have done litter picking. I also got in touch with a local garden centre who have been donating an abundance of plants which the children are now looking after.*

Orange string – multiple meanings. Sometimes I feel like I am literally hanging on by a thread. A very thin and fraying thread. Work situation is very challenging, which has been made extremely hard since contracting Covid. So this orange thread is a representation of just how insecure and unstable my life often feels, HOWEVER, it is also the thread that I have placed running through all of the items on here as this piece of thread is also the connection between everything in my life, both professional and personal. Just like the crystals, the animals, the music, the books, the hands, the jewellery, the bucket... this thread may be frayed, it may be exhausted and hanging ready to snap or drop, but it is also strong and powerful, it makes connections between things and people, it is the thread that keeps on going (I did originally have it still attached to the rest of the ball but my daughter cut it), it is the thread that entwines and interweaves and maintains a strength no matter what and I feel that it represents me and how I feel... a bit of a loose end, very frayed and often wondering if and when I'll snap but hanging on with every tiny fibre and staying strong despite everything.

And finally, rather than placing these items beautifully on a table, I used the trampoline I bought for my girls during first lockdown for fun and movement breaks in between their Google classroom and watching me fight for my life. I chose the trampoline as my table because there's a Tigger in me! Behind the quiet, thoughtful, calm exterior, there is also a very cheeky and bouncy side to me. It's been a long time since I felt 'Tiggerific' but I know it's lurking in there and will never go away. Long Covid will not beat me (hence not putting my endless meds and inhalers that I now rely on, on there... these, I will not let define me).

Although I didn't put a picture of my gorgeous girls on there, they too define me and make me who I am today. They are represented in every item on there in one way or another and if it wasn't for them and my mum, who is also represented throughout, I wouldn't be anywhere near the person I am today or doing what I do. For me the early years are exactly that, they are the foundation for setting up the rest of a life. I've always said, 'You wouldn't build a house on a dodgy foundation so why do it to a child?' This, to me, is the crux of everything I do at work and at home for my girls. A gazillion challenges and hurdles along the way but my string won't snap.

I have read Jessica's reflection repeatedly. For me it shows me how reflective, open, and honest an individual can be when given time, space and a creative method of reflection. Thank you, Jessica.

FIGURE 5.2 Object Orientated Reflection

Your Reflective Space and *Wabi-Sabi*

Having explored what is reflection and reflective theory, and also several creative ways to reflect, it is important to consider your reflective space, where this is and what it looks like. If we return to the word **wabi-sabi** and the **perfectly imperfect** concept, it leads us to consider how as a world we can seek beauty from the imperfect and how much more sustainable this makes us as individuals.

Each new academic year on social media you can find educators posting images of their new classrooms created before the children arrive. You will also find posts of new pens, equipment and resources and this can make others feel overwhelmed by the need to be perfect, and to create the perfect learning environment. If you adopt the **wabi-sabi** approach, you will think and reflect differently about what your own reflective space and this may further lead you to reflect upon the learning environments you provide for your young children and families.

Our world needs help, and we need to seek new ways to help it survive. One way we can do this is by considering the following ***wabi-sabi*** tips as you set out your reflective space:

1. Do you need it? Will it really add any more beauty to the space? Can you be more sustainable? Some objects you have improve with age.
2. Your reflective space does not have to be perfect. Seek out those perfectly imperfect items.
3. Less stuff creates calm.
4. Work with peaceful tones and hues, and with nature tones such as greens, blues and greys.

This is a space where you will create stories, think, be reflective and not drop your standards. Just be ***perfectly imperfect***.

Chapter Reflection

In this chapter, you have been invited to consider several ways to reflect creatively and how to use ***wabi-sabi*** in your reflective space. You may wish to try one creative method a week and you will soon discover which methods work best for you. However, you choose to reflect, and take time to remember these are your stories and your reflections which form part of your reflective, ongoing journey.

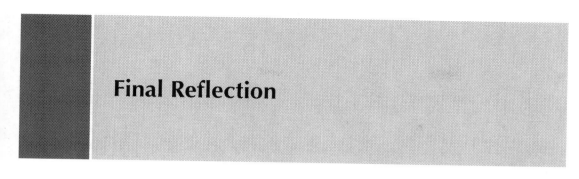

Final Reflection

I wanted to end this book both reflectively and creatively and so I give you another Japanese word: ***Ippitsuryu***.

Ippitsuryu is an ancient Japanese technique of creating the image of the flowing, river-like body of the dragon, achieved by just one single stroke of a brush. If ever you watch an artist using this technique, you will witness and feel the sense of flow as the artist uses the brush to create a smooth flow of pattern and texture.

Our academic, professional and personal lives do not always flow in such a smooth way. Our reflective journey will not always be a smooth one, but taking time to reflect and adopting some of the strategies within my book will support you in your reflective journey.

By reflecting daily, I believe you will find your flow and your inner dragon.

DOI: 10.4324/b23021-6

References

Brookfield, S. (1994) *Becoming a Critically Reflective Teacher*. San Francisco, CA: Jossey-Bass.

Gibbs, G. (1998) *Learning by Doing: A Guide to Teaching and Learning through Reflective Practice*. Oxford: Oxford Brookes University.

Kline, N. (1999) *Time to Think*. London: Cassell.

Kolb, D. (1984) *Experiential Learning as the Science of Learning and Development*. Englewood Cliffs, NJ: Prentice Hall.

Schon, D. A. (1983) *The Reflective Practitioner*. San Francisco, CA: Jossey-Bass.

Index

Index

Printed in the United States
by Baker & Taylor Publisher Services